Possessions and Exorcisms

New and future titles in the series include:
Alien Abductions
Angels
Atlantis
The Bermuda Triangle
The Curse of King Tut
Dragons
Dreams
ESP
The Extinction of the Dinosaurs
Extraterrestrial Life
Fairies
Fortune-Telling
Ghosts
Haunted Houses
Jack the Ripper
The Kennedy Assassination
King Arthur
Life After Death
The Loch Ness Monster
Mysterious Places
Pyramids
Shamans
Stonehenge
UFOs
Unicorns
Vampires
Witches

The Mystery Library

Possessions
and Exorcisms

Stuart A. Kallen

LUCENT BOOKS

An imprint of Thomson Gale, a part of The Thomson Corporation

THOMSON

GALE

Detroit • New York • San Francisco • San Diego • New Haven, Conn. • Waterville, Maine • London • Munich

© 2005 Thomson Gale, a part of The Thomson Corporation.

Thomson and Star Logo are trademarks and Gale and Lucent Books are registered trademarks used herein under license.

For more information, contact
Lucent Books
27500 Drake Rd.
Farmington Hills, MI 48331-3535
Or you can visit our Internet site at http://www.gale.com

LIBRARY OF CONGRESS CATALOGING-IN-PUBLICATION DATA

Kallen, Stuart A., 1955–
    Possessions and exorcisms / by Stuart A. Kallen.
        p. cm. — (The mystery library)
    Includes bibliographical references and index.
    ISBN 1-59018-130-1 (alk. paper)
     1. Demonic possession—Juvenile literature. 2. Exorcism—Juvenile literature.
    I. Title. II. Series: Mystery library (Lucent Books)
    BF1555.K34 2004
    133.4'26—dc22
                                                                            2004010561

Printed in the United States of America

Contents

Foreword

In Shakespeare's immortal play *Hamlet*, the young Danish aristocrat Horatio has clearly been astonished and disconcerted by his encounter with a ghostlike apparition on the castle battlements. "There are more things in heaven and earth," his friend Hamlet assures him, "than are dreamt of in your philosophy."

Many people today would readily agree with Hamlet that the world and the vast universe surrounding it are teeming with wonders and oddities that remain largely outside the realm of present human knowledge or understanding. How did the universe begin? What caused the dinosaurs to become extinct? Was the lost continent of Atlantis a real place or merely legendary? Does a monstrous creature lurk beneath the surface of Scotland's Loch Ness? These are only a few of the intriguing questions that remain unanswered, despite the many great strides made by science in recent centuries.

Lucent Books' Mystery Library series is dedicated to exploring these and other perplexing, sometimes bizarre, and often disturbing or frightening wonders. Each volume in the series presents the best-known tales, incidents, and evidence surrounding the topic in question. Also included are the opinions and theories of scientists and other experts who have attempted to unravel and solve the ongoing mystery. And supplementing this information is a fulsome list of sources for further reading, providing the reader with the means to pursue the topic further.

The Mystery Library will satisfy every young reader's fascination for the unexplained. As one of history's greatest scientists, physicist Albert Einstein, put it:

> The most beautiful thing we can experience is the mysterious. It is the source of all true art and science. He to whom this emotion is a stranger, who can no longer wonder and stand rapt in awe, is as good as dead: his eyes are closed.

What Is Possession?

As long as humans have walked the earth, they have believed in demons, ghosts, deities, and other supernatural entities with great powers. From ancient cultures to modern times, these spirits have been seen in both positive and negative lights. Those possessed by good spirits are said to have divine visions and supernatural powers that allow them to heal the sick, predict the future, and transform the present. In ancient times, those possessed by positive spirits sometimes decided the fates of nations, advising generals to go to war or kings to sign peace treaties.

Average citizens might consult priests or shamans who channeled spirits to find answers to the most mundane questions, such as when to plant a crop or when to get married. In modern times, positive spirit possession in places such as Haiti, Venezuela, Cambodia, India, and elsewhere continues to be utilized on a regular basis by people searching for answers to life's difficult questions.

Positive spirit possession is often believed to counter negative possession. For example, in some cultures sick people, or those with very bad luck, are said to be possessed by negative spirits. These evil or demonic spirits can wound, torment, and sometimes destroy people.

Spirits said to be on demonic missions seem to have no boundaries and may slip into a person at any time. After taking command, these demons ostensibly take control of speech, actions, physical appearance, and bodily functions. This insidious act, known as possession, has been blamed for a host of problems. A person possessed can experience terrible luck, horrid physical pain, frightening mental illness, and even, some would say, eternal damnation.

Possession is said to happen in various ways. Spirits allegedly possess a person through an intermediary, such as a witch or wizard, or swoop into a person's body through food or drink. A person may bring a diabolical spirit upon him- or herself by

Church ministers exorcise a possessed woman. The distorted face is a typical symptom of demonic possession.

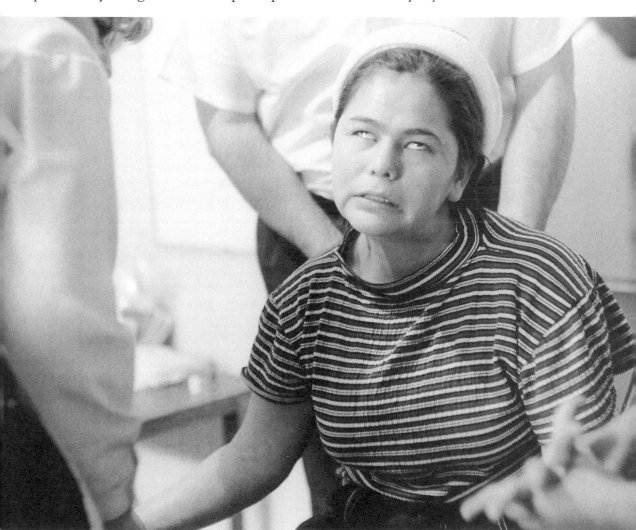

ignoring religious teachings or challenging traditional beliefs. Once possessed, these people often behave in a depraved manner and renounce their god. And anybody can be a victim of possession, from an innocent child to a wicked old man.

In almost all religions people believe in some sort of diabolical possession. Some followers of Judaism fear an entity known as a *dyybuk,* a doomed, ghostlike spirit that can enter a body and cause great physical and mental agony. Some Christians believe people can be possessed by Satan, the ultimate evil entity that can take hold of a person's body and cause him or her to suffer torments, behave oddly, or perform diabolical acts. Some of the frightening symptoms attributed to Satanic possession are discussed by Malachi Martin in *Hostage to the Devil:*

> The stories that are told [about possession] are dramatic and painful: strange physical ailments in the possessed; marked mental derangement; obvious repugnance to all signs, symbols, mention, and sight of religious objects. Often . . . the presence of the [possessed] is marked by so-called psychical phenomena: objects fly around the room; wallpaper peels off the walls; furniture cracks; crockery breaks; there are strange rumblings, hisses, and other noises with no apparent source. Often the temperature in the room where the possessed happens to be will drop dramatically. Even more often an acrid and distinctive stench accompanies the person.[1]

There are other symptoms to possession as well. The face is said to become distorted, with the skin pulled extremely tight so that all lines or wrinkles disappear. Victims are wracked with pain, their breathing may inexplicably stop and start, and the heartbeat becomes barely audible. These afflictions may be accompanied by excessive vomiting, urination, and defecation.

Commanding Demons to an Oath

When a person is supposedly possessed, relatives often seek the help of an exorcist. This person, usually a religious official,

This Renaissance painting depicts an exorcism. The priest uses prayers, blessings, and commands to expel the demon.

performs an exorcism, a ritual that utilizes incantations, commands, or prayer to force the evil spirit to stop afflicting the accursed person.

The word *exorcism* is derived from the Greek word *exorkizein,* which means "to cause to swear an oath." Technically an exorcism does not drive a demon out of a person, but rather it makes the evil spirit swear an oath, or allegiance, to the exorcist. This binds the demon to the exorcist and allows the exorcist's higher authority to control or command the spirit contrary to its own will.

The belief in exorcism is as old as that of spirit possession. As long ago as the fifth century B.C., one of the first records of an exorcism concerned the ghost of a Spartan warrior named Pausanias, who had starved to death in a Greek temple. The hideous songs and shrieks emitted from his ghost petrified worshippers until a holy man drove the warrior's ghost from the temple.

Since that time, numerous exorcisms have been recorded throughout the world including Africa, Latin America, the Middle East, and Asia. In the United States, the Catholic Church has at least ten official exorcists. Protestant sects also believe in satanic possession and exorcism. Some religious researchers believe that there are more than one thousand evangelical Protestant exorcists in the United States today.

Mental or Physical Illness

As long as there have been exorcisms, there have been skeptics who try to dispel the notion of demonic or spirit possession. These nonbelievers point to a number of conditions that may cause a victim to appear possessed. Obvious conditions of mental illness, such as schizophrenia and hysteria, may cause delusions, hallucinations, sleepwalking, and other unusual behavior. These illnesses were virtually unnamed and unknown to laymen before the late nineteenth century. Some have attributed aberrant behavior to food poisoning. Researchers point to a fungus, called ergot, that grows on rye, a grain commonly used for bread in Europe and elsewhere. Used as a base for the powerful hallucinogenic drug LSD, ergot can cause paranoia and hallucinations, twitches and spasms, cardiovascular trouble, and stillbirths—all symptoms attributed to demonic possession.

Finally, there is the power of group suggestion. Children and adults who are easily manipulated may believe that they are harboring demonic spirits when someone such as a priest or parent tells them so. The authority figures may offer clues on how the subject should behave and reward the possessed when he or she lets go of the devil. Known as communal reinforcement, this is believed to be the most common occurrence in modern exorcism rituals.

Whether or not skeptics are correct, possessions and exorcisms have played a long and puzzling role in human history. Some believe possession may be caused by mental or physical illness, while others are convinced that the devil is at work in the mortal world. Whatever the case, possessions and exorcisms remain mysterious forces whose true natures remain unknown.

Chapter 1

Spirit Possession Throughout History

Possession has long been a part of religious rituals in many cultures and is not always associated with negative concepts such as demons and devils. There are thousands of historical records concerning people possessed by "good" spirits. This type of possession is seen as one of the most readily available ways that an average person can form a union with a divine power.

Some people believe it is possible to seek, that is, voluntarily bring a spirit into their body. Those seeking voluntary possession attempt positive possession through a variety of methods. They achieve an altered state of consciousness through rituals, fasting, and self-hypnosis, or even by taking a variety of mind-altering drugs such as peyote or psychedelic mushrooms. Whatever the catalyst, after entering a trance the possessed may feel as if a spirit or deity has taken over his or her mind and body. Sometimes the person has no memory of the experience when it ends. Many times the person's words and actions are recorded by observers and interpreted by religious leaders.

Oracles of a Sun God

While possessed by a benevolent spirit, a person may pass on incredible wisdom or predict the future. This was the case in ancient Greece from the sixth century B.C. to the fourth century A.D., when it was believed that women known as oracles were possessed by the sun god Apollo. Because Apollo was also

This drawing of the oracle at Delphi shows the spirit-possessed Pythia delivering her prophecy. The oracle functioned for centuries.

called Pythius, every oracle was named Pythia, the feminine pronunciation of the sun god's name. Dressed in robes and laurel crowns, the Pythia dispensed predictions about war, peace, revolutions, and even love and marriage, to kings, queens, and average citizens who believed the women were mouthpieces for the divine Apollo.

The behavior of the oracles could be quite odd. This may be seen in a description by a philosopher named Apollonius of Tyana who wrote about an oracle operating from a temple near the city of Delphi in the second century A.D.: "[Pythia's] chest swelled; first she flushed, then paled; her limbs trembled convulsively and more and more violently. Her eyes seemed to flash fire; she foamed at the mouth; her hair stood on end. Then . . . she uttered a few words, which the priests at her side noted down."[2]

The accuracy of the Delphic oracles was legendary. In one famous incident around 480 B.C. the oracles advised Greek leaders—against their better judgment—to fight Persian invaders in a naval battle at the seaport of Salamis. The advice was correct, and the Greek fleet overcame the Persian fleet, which led to the defeat and withdrawal of the Persians from Greece.

Such predictions attracted the rich and powerful from many nations during the next ten centuries that the oracles existed. All seekers at Delphi were required to pay two days' wages and make offerings to the oracles. At its height, these gifts made the shrine one of the richest in the world. In *They Foresaw the Future*, Justine Glass provides examples of the wealth of Delphi:

> [Kings] and princes and humble folk came from far and near . . . with the common hope that their problems would be solved and their future foretold. . . . The wealth and the [objects of art] amassed at Delphi were fabulous. In its temples and theater were golden and marble statues, whose number grew with the fame and prosperity of the place—carvings, jewels, paintings, . . . golden cups and platters, everything that symbolized opulence was to be found there.[3]

These riches reflected the donors' belief that the predictions handed down by Apollo through the oracles were accurate. Even the Roman philosopher Cicero, who was a skeptic about possession, had to admit that "the oracle of Delphi [never could] have been so overwhelmed with so many important offerings from monarch and nations if all the ages had not proved the truth of its oracles."[4]

As far back as the fourth century B.C., however, skeptics tried to explain—beyond spirit possession—the flushed faces and convulsions experienced by the Delphic oracles. The Greek historian Herodotus claimed that volcanic gases, emitted from cracks in the cave floor, had hallucinogenic effects on the women. It is unknown where Herodotus acquired this information, but a 2001 study by a team of geologists uncovered traces of a volcanic gas called ethylene, which has a sweet smell and produces a narcotic effect described as a floating or disembodied euphoria. This toxic gas may have been responsible for nearly ten centuries of prophesy by the possessed oracles.

Christian Possession

Whatever the cause of their altered states, oracles fell out of favor around the fifth century A.D. when Christianity became well established in Greece. Possession in early Christianity was seen as communing with the Holy Spirit, a very positive thing. And the most common method of expressing possession was known as glossolalia, or "speaking in tongues." This is a phenomenon in which the believer, in an ecstatic state of possession, speaks in a foreign language or utters unintelligible sounds that are taken to contain divine messages. The first mention of this practice was at Pentecost, or the celebration seven weeks after Passover. It was recorded in the New Testament Acts 2:4 that the apostles "were filled with the Holy Spirit and began to speak with other tongues, as the Spirit gave them utterance."

This method of possession has long been controversial among believers. Some speakers in tongues believe that they have been singled out as chosen people to take direct action

The Integrity of the Oracles

In ancient Greece there was little doubt that the oracles of Delphi were truly possessed by Apollo. This fact was examined in 1833 by German author P. Stengel, who called the oracles "the Pythoness." His work is reprinted in T.K. Oesterreich's *Possession Demoniacal & Other:*

> Owing to the gaseous emanations arising from the gulf, the Pythoness was thrown into an ecstasy. She then pronounced more or less consecutive words which were rendered by the priests into often very bad [lines of verse] . . . and imparted to the questioners. Sometimes the replies were given in prose. The Pythoness must often have found herself in a state which rendered her incapable of reasoning, and it was then the duty of the priests to see what they could make of her words and outcries.

But deliberate fraud was certainly rare. It may have occurred in isolated cases and a Pythoness is even reported to have been deprived of her office because she was alleged, on receipt of a bribe, to have given a false oracle. But in the hey-day of the oracles the Pythoness and the priests themselves believed, as a general rule, that the god [possessed] her; and even if these men, wily, and for the most part well-informed as to the circumstances of the questioners, showed moreover all possible circumspection and were content to speak darkly and ambiguously where not sure of their ground, it would be impossible to explain the extraordinary regard which the oracle enjoyed for centuries by an attempt to posit repeated fraud.

for the Holy Spirit. But even Saint Paul, the foremost leader of early Christianity, was worried about the phenomenon and found it necessary on one occasion to tell astonished onlookers that the possessed Christians were not drunk. After this experience, according to Corinthians 1:14, Saint Paul lectured the Christians: "If therefore, the whole church assembles, and all speak in tongues, and outsiders or unbelievers enter, will they not say that you are mad?"

For this reason, church authorities in later centuries stated that the genuine gift of tongues was limited to the earliest days of Christianity. The practice was revived in the nineteenth century, however, by Mormons, Methodists, and some Presbyterians. In the 1830s and 1840s the Shaker worshippers created prayers and hymns in tongues while possessed by the Holy Spirit. Because the prayers and hymns were in unknown languages, they were written down phonetically.

Today some believe that worshippers may speak in tongues following conversion to Christianity. Skeptics, however, explain the phenomenon as a hypnotic trance that results from religious excitement. As psychiatrist William Sargant writes in *The Mind Possessed:*

> The gift of tongues is still present and observable in various religious movements. All cases, when carefully examined, seem to be typical hysterical . . . phenomena, and there is really nothing to suggest that the early Christian speaking in tongues was anything different.[5]

The Devil's New Powers

To believers, those speaking in tongues were possessed by God. In the Middle Ages, however, religious leaders who wanted to

Christ confronts Satan in this medieval illumination. Medieval Christians believed God and the devil fought over people's souls.

halt the practice accused those who spoke in tongues of demonic possession.

By this time, the belief that the devil could take possession of a person's body had been long established. Demonic possession is mentioned in the New Testament dozens of times. As Christianity became the dominant religion of Europe in the Middle Ages, it was said that a demon, in the form of Satan, emerged as the prime adversary of God and His works. Most medieval Christians believed that there was a constant war being waged between God and the devil for peoples' souls.

By the fourteenth century, the devil's elevated stature elicited a wave of hysteria that swept across Europe. This all-powerful spirit was said to be responsible for all that was bad, from plagues and wars to crop failures and natural disasters. The description of the devil's powers by sixteenth-century religious scholar Johann Weaver was typical of the beliefs during this time:

> Satan possess a great courage, incredible cunning, superhuman wisdom, the most accurate penetrations, consummate prudence, an incomparable skill in veiling the most pernicious artifices [deceptions] under a specious disguise and a malefic [malicious] and infinite hatred towards the human race. [6]

Such descriptions were used to strike fear into the hearts of average citizens in order to encourage loyalty to the Church. But no matter how real religious leaders tried to make Satan, according to Roger Baker in *Binding the Devil*, "he was not, like a stag or a bear, visible to be chased and slaughtered. He could only be isolated when he chose to make his presence known through the behaviour of some unfortunate individual he had chosen to possess." [7]

Ways in Which Demons Took Possession

When the devil possessed a person, the victim was said to become a demonic entity. It was believed that his or her behavior changed completely. In reality, this often meant that anyone displaying odd or unusual conduct was suspected of being possessed by the devil. Even unusual birthmarks, warts, or moles were suspected of being signs of "the devil's mark."

Other signs of possession included displays of lewd and obscene behavior, obsessive sexual thoughts, horrible body odors or the smell of sulfur, a distended stomach, and abnormal body strength and insensitivity to pain. Possessed persons were also said to express revulsion to holy things, especially the reading of Scripture or contact with holy water or other blessed objects such as the cross. Perhaps most frightening were changes in the vocal chords that reduced someone's voice to a rasping, guttural bark said to be the voice of the devil.

Certain religious scholars, called demonologists, believed that there were several ways devils could possess someone. Either the devil passed directly into a victim without the person's permission, or a person could volunteer his or her body to Satan. More commonly, it was said that a witch or wizard collaborated with the devil to take control of a person through bewitchment. Victims of this act were called demoniacs.

Oftentimes devil possessions involved children who were allegedly accursed by old women. For example, in 1598, in Jura, Switzerland, an eight-year-old named Loyse Maillat became suddenly paralyzed. Her parents took her to a church where the priest announced Maillat was possessed by five demons the child named "Wolf," "Cat," "Dog," "Jolly," and "Griffon." In *Heresy, Magic, and Witchcraft in Early Modern Europe,* Gary K. Waite picks up the story:

> When the priest asked the girl who had cast the spell on her, she pointed to one of the spectators, Françoise Secretain, an old woman who the night before the fits started had requested a night's lodging of Loyse's mother, who initially refused because her husband was away but finally succumbed to Françoise's pleas. While the mother was momentarily absent the visitor supposedly compelled the girl to eat a piece of bread "resembling dung." The next day Loyse was possessed. . . . [8]

The Witch's Hammer

Malleus Maleficarum (The Witch's Hammer), first published in 1486, was a handbook used by demonologists and witch hunters to identify, persecute, and execute witches and others believed to be possessed by the devil. In the following passage, the authors, two German Dominican friars, Heinrich Krämer and Jakob Sprenger, describe ways the devil may possess a victim:

> [Some] are affected only in their own bodies; some both in their bodies and in their inner perceptions; some only in their inner perceptions; some are so punished as to be at times only deprived of their reason; and others are turned into the semblance of irrational beasts. . . .

> We may mention an example. . . . A certain priest was possessed, and during an exorcism the devil was asked for how long he had inhabited that priest. He answered, For seven years. And when the exorcist objected, But you have tormented him for hardly three years; where were you for the rest of the time? He answered, I was hiding in his body. And when he asked in what part of the body, he answered, Generally in his head. And when he was again asked where he was when the priest was celebrating the Sacrament, he said, I hid myself under his tongue. . . .

> And so the devil occupied the body of the priest. . . . First, as he could enter his body within its physical limits, so he occupied his head by substantially inhabiting it. Secondly, he could extrinsically work upon his reason. And he could have so tormented him without any intermission or respite. . . . And in these ways devils can without doubt at the instance of witches and with God's permission inflict torments.

If Secretain did indeed cause demons to possess the little girl, she had committed a very serious crime. The priest reported this to government authorities. Secretain was arrested and hauled before a judge named Henri Bogue, the author of *Discours des Sorciers* (*Speeches of the Sorcerers*), a book that drew connections between demonic possession and witchcraft. Although Secretain was known throughout the town to be a devout Christian who prayed the rosary constantly, the judge used mental and physical torture to extract a confession from the woman. She was then convicted of witchcraft, tortured, and burned at the stake.

Secretain was among the one hundred thousand alleged witches who were executed in Europe between 1450 and 1700. In her case and many others, however, the demoniacs themselves were treated with mercy because they did not ask to associate with the devil. In *Unclean Spirits,* D.P. Walker draws the distinction between witches and their victims, and how they were treated differently by authorities:

> The devil is not inside a witch's body, as he is in a demoniac's; in consequence a witch does not suffer from convulsions and a demoniac does. A witch has voluntarily entered into association with a devil, whereas possession is involuntary and a demoniac is not therefore responsible for her wicked actions, as is a witch.[9]

Whether a person was suspected of witchcraft or possession, it was not unusual for religious authorities to consult doctors to evaluate the situation. Medieval physicians used their rudimentary knowledge of natural diseases to determine if the symptoms were possibly caused by physical or mental illness.

While doctors and demonologists attempted to determine the causes of diabolical possession, it was politics that drove the hysteria. Historians believe that witch hunts had less to do with demoniacs than with profound divisions within the Christian Church. Fear of Satanic possession reached its peak during the Reformation, which began in 1517 when the Protestant sect broke away from the Roman Catholic Church. In places such as Switzerland and Germany, where these splits were most contentious, accusations of demonic possession were highest. As religious groups fought to spread their beliefs among the public, they competed with one another to see who could be more righteous. This often entailed persecuting large numbers of alleged witches and devil worshippers. The victims, caught in the middle of the religious schism, were often the poorest and most vulnerable members of society. A full 80 percent were women.

Voluntary Possession

By the 1750s, belief in demonology was fading in Europe. It was an era known as the Age of Enlightenment, and scientists regularly published popular books that exposed accusations of devil possession as overblown, irrational, and barbarous. The idea of spirit possession did not go away, however, but began to manifest itself in a more benign form called ghost possession.

The belief in ghosts—spirits of the dead who appear in visible form—is as old and as universal as the belief in demons. Some believe that certain people, called mediums, oracles, or soothsayers, have the ability to communicate with ghosts. This happens when a medium voluntarily "channels" a spirit of the dead in order to allow it to possess his or her body. The ghost may then express its desires through the medium by a process called automatic writing, in which the ghost takes control of the channeler to jot down words or pictures.

With automatic writing, the medium goes into a trance-like state and purportedly allows the ghost to deliver a message by moving a pen in his or her hand. Those who perform automatic writing say they are most often unaware that it is happening. Such writing takes place very quickly, and words tend

This drawing depicts the execution of suspected witches. Witches were believed to cause demonic possession.

to be strung together or even illegible. The handwriting is often different from the writer's normal style and sometimes is said to resemble the handwriting of the dead person being channeled. In extreme cases, automatic writers produce backward script that must be read in a mirror or writing in a foreign language unknown to the channeler.

In the 1850s automatic writing gained widespread popularity when a medium named John Worth Edmonds was allegedly possessed by the spirit of seventeenth-century English

A woman in a trance performs automatic writing. Some people believe a spirit writes via the possessed person.

24

philosopher Francis Bacon. Edmonds claimed that Bacon's ghost took control of his hand and used automatic writing to communicate mystical messages. Critics pointed out, however, that the writings were pompous, boring, bland, and totally unlike the actual writings of the philosophical genius. Despite the criticism, people bought Edmonds' books, which inspired others to create commercial works in this manner. With the financial success of Edmonds, automatic writing became a fad that swept through Europe and the United States.

Dozens of people capitalized on the automatic-writing sensation. One of the most famous was Swiss-born Hélène Smith, who gained notoriety in the 1890s by claiming to channel the spirit of eighteenth-century magician Leopold Cagliostro. When Cagliostro supposedly took possession of Smith— usually in front of a large audience—the medium's appearance changed to resemble that of the deceased magician. During these sessions, Smith claimed that Cagliostro transported her to Mars. These journeys resulted in automatic writing in which Smith wrote cryptic missives said to be in the Martian alphabet and drew childlike pictures of Martian landscapes that included plants, houses, and city streets.

Smith had many followers and was also subject to an investigation by Swiss psychologist Théodore Flournoy, who watched the medium channel Cagliostro for five years. Flournoy believed that Smith's was a rare case because, unlike many mediums who do not remember the possession experience, Smith remained conscious while channeling Cagliostro. During these episodes, Flournoy wrote that Smith

> told me more than once that she had the impression of becoming, and of momentarily being, Leopold. . . . [He] seems to pass gradually into her, she feels him . . . invade and penetrate her whole substance as if he became herself or she him. It is . . . spontaneous incarnation without loss of consciousness or memory. . . . These hybrid states in which the consciousness and powers of reflection of the normal self persist while

the second personality takes possession of the organism are of extreme interest. [10]

Flournoy concluded that the medium was not possessed. Instead he believed that Smith had a vivid imagination—and possibly a split personality. Flournoy published his findings in *From India to the Planet Mars: A Study of a Case of Somnambulism with Glossolalia,* in 1900. Although the book's conclusion reflected negatively on Smith, the exposure only helped increase the medium's popularity.

Automatic Speech

Smith also claimed to channel Cagliostro's voice and speech patterns when she was possessed by his spirit. This phenom-

Possessed by a Dead Magician

Medium Hélène Smith claimed to channel the spirit of famed eighteenth-century magician Leopold Cagliostro, who allegedly transported her to Mars. When possessed by Cagliostro, Smith's body seemed to undergo remarkable transformations, described by Swiss psychologist Théodore Flournoy in his 1900 study of Smith, *From India to Planet Mars: A Study of a Case of Somnambulism with Glossolalia:*

It is only slowly and step by step that Leopold (Cagliostro) succeeds in [possessing Hélène]. Hélène at first feels as if her arms were seized or did not exist . . . her eyelids droop, the expression of her face changes and her throat swells into a sort of double chin which gives her a kind of family resemblance to the well-known picture of Cagliostro. Suddenly she rises, then turning slowly towards the person in the audience to whom Leopold is about to address himself. . . . Soon, after a series of hiccups, sighs, and various sounds showing the difficulty which Leopold experiences in taking possession of vocal organs, then comes speech, grave, slow and powerful, a man's strong bass voice, slightly thick, with a foreign pronunciation and a marked accent which is certainly rather Italian than anything else. Leopold is not always very easy to understand, especially when his thunderous voice swells and rolls at some indiscreet question or the disrespectful remarks of a [skeptical] onlooker. He stammers, lisps . . . [and] sprinkles his vocabulary with obsolete words or others unsuited to the occasion. He is pompous, unctuous, grandiloquent, sometimes severe and terrible, but also sentimental. . . . When she (Hélène) incarnates her guide, she really takes on a certain facial resemblance to him, and her whole bearing has something theatrical, sometimes really majestic which is entirely consistent with what may be imagined of the real Cagliostro.

enon, known as automatic speech, was practiced by many mediums who alleged that ghosts had taken possession of their vocal chords in order to speak to onlookers. Although the process of automatic speech is similar to speaking in tongues, the speakers are more readily understood by listeners. And some of those capable of automatic speech can be amazingly prolific. This was the case with St. Louis housewife Pearl Curran.

In 1913 Curran claimed that she was often possessed by the ghost of Patience Worth, a seventeenth-century farm woman who was killed in an Indian attack. While in possession of Curran, Worth was able to speak to the living. Although Curran had only an eighth-grade education, when she was possessed by Worth's spirit, she created an amazing body of work that was written down by a friend as it was dictated. This included twenty-nine volumes consisting of twenty-five hundred poems, six full-length historical novels, plus plays, short stories, and other writings. These works enjoyed widespread popularity in the second decade of the twentieth century.

In all, Curran, while in a trance, dictated more than 4 million words—about sixteen thousand pages—in little more than five years. These creations have been analyzed by scholars who found the details historically accurate and the plots and characters amazingly well constructed. Those who challenge the concept of automatic speech say that while Curran's output was highly unusual, she must have been dictating stories from her subconscious. Others point out, however, that some of the stories were written with an authentic Old English vocabulary that Curran would have no way of knowing. Whatever the case, after seven years Curran claimed that Worth stopped talking to her, and the automatic speech came to an end.

"All Belief Is for It"
Automatic speech is but one of the many ways people claim to channel spirits. Throughout history thousands have asserted that they were possessed by gods, ghosts, demons, and other

spirits. Although skeptics try to trace possession to mental illness, self-fulfilling prophesy, religious hysteria, or outright fraud, declarations of spirit possession come from many cultures. While science has never been able to prove that spirit possession is real, it has also been unable to state that it is not real. Perhaps eighteenth-century author Samuel Johnson, who was one of the most respected intellectuals of his time, best summed up the situation when he told a friend about human interaction with ghostly spirits, saying: "All argument is against it; but all belief is for it."[11]

Chapter 2

Worldwide Possession

History is rife with episodes of alleged spirit possession, and belief in possession is still popular in many cultures throughout the world today. From the Caribbean to Cambodia to the South American rain forests, innumerable people believe that their minds and bodies can be controlled by spirits. These spirits are largely positive and have a constructive role to play in society. And those who channel spirits are often revered by others and sought out for advice.

Spirits take possession of the living through various means, including dancing, drumming, and singing. This repetitive activity induces what is called a "possession trance." When this semihypnotized state is achieved, gods and spirits are said to enter the participants and direct their actions and speech. These animating forces might be animal spirits, gods, ancient ancestors, or other supernatural entities.

Possessed by Voodoo Spirits

In Haiti a large majority of the people practice vodou, or voodoo. This religion is named for the word *vodun*, which means "spirit" in the Dahomean language of West Africa. The religion fuses some Catholic beliefs with the practices of several traditional African ethnic groups such as the Ibos, Dahomeans, Congos, Senegalese, Libyans, and Ethiopians. Some of the traditions are said to be more than ten thousand years old.

Practitioners of voodoo, or voodooists, believe that a god called Gran Mèt created heaven and earth. Too powerful and magnificent to bother with the mundane daily desires of human beings, Gran Mèt also created hundreds of spirits called loa to act as his intermediaries on earth. These deities are said to rule many vital forces of life. For example, Agaou is the loa of thunder, Yoruba is the loa of warfare, Ogoun is the loa of war and thunderbolts, Erzulie is the loa of love, Agwé is the loa of water and the ocean, and Azacca is the loa of agriculture.

In order to obtain the wisdom and blessings of the spirits, voodooists consult with the loa before they engage in any important activities such as marriage, moving, or planting crops. To do so, they pray, sing, and dance until a possession trance ensues. During this activity, the loa are said to enter the bodies of the voodooists and "ride" them like "horses." For this reason, voodooists refer to spirit possession as being ridden as a spirit horse.

"Master of the Head"

Many voodooists are first ridden as spirit horses during adolescence. The possession may initially occur either spontaneously, from stress, or while attending drum and dance ceremonies. When a youngster does experience the first possession, the particular loa that rode him or her is identified and discussed with relatives. A brief initiation ceremony is held to please the residing loa, which is then said to be the "master of the head" of the voodooist.

Once someone becomes the horse of a particular loa, he or she will practice certain rituals or perform specific songs and dances. Such rituals put the voodooist into a state of possession trance, which allows the spirits to enter them. During these ceremonies a string of other spirits may take possession of the voodooist temporarily, but only with permission of the "master of the head." Each loa has its own characteristics, and the possessed will act out roles determined by the spirit. For example, those possessed by the snake god Dumballah will

Ridden by the Spirits

Possession is a central feature of Haitian voodoo ceremonies. Believers say that specific deities, called loa, "ride" the bodies of the worshippers during ceremonies. William Sargant describes a ceremony of spirit possession in his book *The Mind Possessed:*

> The dancing and drumming went on hour after hour and every sort of loa appeared [to take possession of those in attendance] at one time or another. We saw the Dumballah, the snake god, and the person possessed by him behaved like a snake. At a later service at the same place we saw somebody possessed by Dumballah climbing into the rafters of the roof as a snake might do. . . . We saw, among others, Erszuli, goddess of love, Baron Samedi, keeper of the graveyard, and Agwe, goddess of the sea. [Warrior god] Ogoun also

appeared and Ghede . . . god of the phallus. When Ghede descends and takes possession, he often exhibits very erotic behaviour as a challenge to the respectability of some of the visitors.

What was perfectly clear from these exciting few hours was that the various possession states provide an outlet for every type of normal and abnormal behaviour among people whose lives are one long struggle against poverty and despair. We saw them becoming gods, behaving like gods, and for a while forgetting all their troubles. After the ceremony was over they were quite convinced that for a time, despite their humility and poverty on earth, they had been one with the gods themselves. Life had regained purpose and dignity for them.

Loa-possessed voodoo practitioners dance during a ceremony. They believe loa ride them like horses.

slither around on the floor like a snake while hissing and flicking the tongue.

Voodoo practitioners develop a working rapport with their loa, who are said to agree not to ride them when it is not desired. Those who cannot control their loa are thought to be mentally ill and in need of healing from a special voodoo doctor. Erika Bourguignon explains in her book *Possession:*

> This is a two-way relationship, in which the human "horse" is expected to gain increasing knowledge and with this, increasing control over the appearance of the spirits. In fact, elderly people are rarely possessed, because, it is said, they have gained much knowledge and because the spirits are considerate in not imposing the fatigue of a possession trance, with its dancing and sometimes acrobatics, on the elderly.[12]

The Possession-Trance Ceremony

Possession-trance ceremonies are often the most significant events in the lives of Haitians, many of whom lead extremely difficult lives of poverty and despair. There are about thirty voodoo holidays every year—up to three in some months—and many of them are dedicated to specific loa. During these holidays, trance rituals become public spectacles in every city and village. Dozens of people experience possession while hundreds of bystanders watch.

The ceremonies begin with prayer and the music of steel drums, gourd rattles, and other percussion instruments. Catholic prayers are mixed with specific prayers to loa as participants dance in an increasingly frenzied manner until they become horses for the loa. Bourguignon describes the experience at a ceremony held in a rural voodoo church:

> Several women seemed to fall, losing their balance, one rolling on the ground. . . . At that moment about 100 to 150 people were tightly packed under the shelter,

around . . . the drum. . . . Outside [the shelter] about the fire a large crowd had gathered, mainly younger people and children and a few women with trays filled with cold drinks and edibles of various sorts which they were offering for sale. Inside . . . the drum . . . continued, as well as new possessions. [A voodooist named] Sino, a little man usually humble and deferential, was possessed by [the nature loa] Papa Loko. He now acted like a royalty, full of dignity and ceremony. After several hours of . . . continuous possessions, the crowd gradually drifted outside. . . . Finally the drums moved out, and then [voodooists] Augusta, Josilia, and a group of other women, now dressed . . . [as] corpses, cotton in their mouths and nostrils, uttering unearthly groans. They were possessed by Maît' Cimtié, the master of the cemetery. As soon as the drums started, they began to dance [through] the fire, but actually although it must have been rather hot, without any real violence or any real danger of burning. [13]

The described ceremony lasted until dawn, at which time, the loa were said to have departed. Although they were gone, some people continued their trance dances well into the next day.

Sometimes those experiencing possession may offer to share divine advice with bystanders. They may predict the future in response to questions from observers or offer tips for gathering wealth or attracting love.

There are also many evil spirits in voodoo, and some of them are said to cause disease. Those possessed by loa with healing powers may perform a ritual called *pase poul,* literally "pass the chicken," to drive off such evil spirits. The healers rub live chickens or doves on the bodies of the sick. After the evil spirits are allegedly transferred to the chicken, the bird is grasped by the neck and whirled around until its head twists off. In a nation with only one doctor per twelve thousand people, this spiritual healing is often the only hope for the ill and dying.

A voodoo priestess performs the pase poul *ritual on a man using a dove. The ritual is done to drive off evil spirits.*

While voodooists firmly believe that such possessions are real, scientists and anthropologists have studied the Haitian possession-trance phenomena and have come to other conclusions. Given the harsh circumstances of most Haitians' daily lives, loa possession is said to give a psychological boost to people who cannot find personal satisfaction elsewhere. By masquerading as potent spirits, people acting as spirit horses can boast of a power otherwise unavailable. In addition, spirit possession allows them to forget their problems for a night and dance with the divine. As psychiatrist Sargant writes:

> Your god comes to you, possesses you, mounts you, and you become a god yourself. And these very humble peo-

ple, with very humble lives, are enabled thereby to live lives of comparative happiness because they have found a religion which does bring down their gods to them. And their gods live in them and they live in their gods. For that reason they are very much happier people than many of us who search for God and never find him, and whose conception of God is some intellectual process conceived in some vague manner in which his God is above, miles and miles away. To them their gods are real.[14]

Famous Spirits from History

The loa of Haiti are deities that hold great power over nature and the lives of people. Not all possession sects channel gods, however. In central Venezuela, the 2 million members of the cult of Maria Lionza claim to be possessed by spirits of famous figures from Venezuelan history.

According to legend, Maria Lionza was the daughter of a Spanish conquistador and a princess from one of the indigenous Indian tribes. Lionza is sometimes portrayed as a powerful and attractive Indian woman, nude and muscular, riding a tapir and lifting to heaven a pelvic bone, the symbol of fertility. In another guise, Lionza appears as a virginal young girl similar in appearance to the Virgin Mary, after whom she is named. Also known as "the Queen," Maria Lionza is said to rule a kingdom of spirits on Mount Sorte, near Maria Lionza National Park about two hundred miles from Caracas.

The mountain is said to be home to the spirits of legendary characters from Venezuelan history. The most popular is Simón Bolívar, a Venezuelan revolutionary leader of the early nineteenth century who fought the Spanish to gain independence for present-day Venezuela, Colombia, Ecuador, Peru, and Bolivia. Other spirits included "El Negro Felipe," a black man who fought with Bolívar, "El Indio Guaicaipuro," an Indian who was said to battle against the Spanish conquistadors in the sixteenth century, and Jose Gregorio Hernandez, a popular Venezuelan doctor. In addition, there are various Indian spirits who are believed to have lived in the area in the centuries before the Spanish conquest.

Through trance-possession ceremonies that include singing, dancing, and drumming, these spirits can take possession of human mediums. Large audiences gather around the channelers in order to listen to what the spirits have to say. According to the beliefs of the Maria Lionza sect, the spirits occupy the earth, just as humans do. The walls of houses and other barriers obstruct spirit possession, however, so mediums perform

This devotee of the Maria Lionza sect is possessed by a departed spirit. The Venezuelan cult has 2 million followers.

The Spirits Speak

The 2 million members of the cult of Maria Lionza believe that when individual spirits possess mediums, each speaks in its own specific way. Barbara Placido explains in "It's All to Do with Words: An Analysis of Spirit Possession in the Venezuelan Cult of Maria Lionza," from the *Journal of the Royal Anthropological Institute:*

> Human relations with the spirits are all [centered] around communication and constructed through words, and spirits themselves are defined by the ways they speak. Every single spirit is characterized by the way he or she speaks and by what he or she says. One can always recognize [the spirit named] el Negro Felipe because he speaks with no "I." La Negra Francisca, a very popular and much-loved spirit, is loud and vulgar. She is a very sexy character and when she descends she likes to talk about men and sex. She defines herself . . . a whore. When she descends she flirts with men and she tells women to have fun, to dance, flirt and sing, but she also always tells them "do not end up a whore like me." Maria Lionza in contrast, speaks with a very soft and low voice and always starts by repeating at least one "general message," "a message that touches everybody's heart," as [a believer named] Lourdes says. "She uses a very learned language and says 'Let us not make money into a god. It is possible to buy a cross, but not salvation. Do not make promiscuity a god.' But she can also be very humble," Lourdes adds, "and says things like 'I am only one of the servants of the army of spirits that God has to help you.'"

their rituals in wilderness areas such as forests and along river banks. Although the spirits cannot cure physical ailments, those who attend believe they can offer advice concerning luck, love, wealth, and continued good health.

Communication with the spirits is very important to members of the cult, as Barbara Placido explains in the *Journal of the Royal Anthropological Institute:*

> Mediums and believers value the content of the episodes very highly and often tape [record] all the possession episodes in order to listen to them over and over again. For example, [a believer named] Lourdes . . . has been taping everything that the spirits say to her since she started going to visit them at the mountain. She spends many evenings listening to these tapes together with her family and friends, and she also writes down what the spirits have been saying in a notebook. These

tape-listening sessions are very interesting occasions. When the spirits are present people focus on them; while they listen to the tapes, they explain, remember, add information, and comment on what the spirits say. Many mediums and believers actually remember by heart some of the most frequent and most interesting phrases of the spirits. . . . [And the spirits] love talking. In fact they are desperate to speak because, mediums and believers insist, spirits need to speak in order to "exist." The idea that the spirits could be wandering around without being able to express themselves is a cause of great worry and distress for many of those who believe in them. [15]

When spirits take possession of mediums, they can offer advice targeted at specific individuals or even at other spirits allegedly present. The advice may concern a person's health, economic situation, or family problems. It is imperative that the humans follow and obey the spirits' words of wisdom. If the advice is not followed, the spirits become agitated and refuse to descend when the people want to speak to them in the future.

The spirits also offer moral messages. For example, the spirits offer guidance to married couples who are having problems, telling them not to divorce. They warn teenage girls to remain virgins until marriage and advise boys to treat women with respect. As Placido writes:

> [Spirits] are not there simply to give advice on specific matters, but also to tell people how they should lead their lives, to teach them about what is proper and what is good. . . . It is about learning how to live; spiritualism, mediums and believers often repeat, is a way of life. . . . Spirits do not spell out how people should behave and they do not cure specific illnesses; but they give general messages and tell people about themselves, about their own lives; it is then up to the humans to interpret, understand, and follow.

Spirits . . . often affirm that the mountain, the cult, their beliefs, and their practices are about beauty and purity, about order and morality, about becoming clean and behaving properly. It is of this pureness and morality that the spirits speak. [16]

While some doubt that the spirits of Maria Lionza or Simón Bolívar are actually inhabiting the bodies of mediums, the counseling offered by those allegedly possessed is beneficial to members of the sect. And for those who make the pilgrimage to the wilderness around Mount Sorte, the positive message they can take home with them on tape recordings helps them cope in their daily lives.

A Venezuelan medium channels a spirit for a man seeking protection from his enemies. The channeled spirits offer advice on many topics.

Channeling Religious, Mythical, and Animal Spirits

Half a world away, in the Southeast Asian country of Cambodia, powerful spirits are also said to take possession of mediums. These Cambodian spirits are called *boramey*. There are about ten thousand *boramey* in Cambodia. As in other sects, when a medium is possessed by a *boramey*, his or her character is transformed by the spirit. Such identities can cross gender lines. For example, a princess spirit can possess a male medium.

A Cambodian woman requests good health from a sacred ox said to be possessed by a spirit. Cambodians believe in many types of spirits.

The Cambodians say there are many types of *boramey*, including religious, mythological, and animal spirits. The religious figures come from the rich and complex narratives of

Buddhism, based on the teachings of Buddha that advocate self-denial and universal brotherhood. *Boramey* such as Parvati and Srey Khmeu are divinities who are members of Buddha's family or his original disciples. Others are hermits who possess special spiritual wisdom. Some are hermit monks; others are intellectual hermits.

Many *boramey* channeled by mediums are princes, princesses, kings, and queens. One of the most popular, Preah Kum Long, is a king of legend who suffered from leprosy. As Didier Bertrand writes in *Asian Folklore Studies:* "Preah Kum Long is a curious and playful *boramey*. He often tells sexual and vulgar jokes, and reveals lottery numbers in a comical way. He is so popular that he is considered to be a divine being but most people address him in a more familiar way as 'grandfather.'"[17]

The most prominent *boramey* that possess mediums are several types of dragons that represent various important figures in Cambodian or Buddhist mythology. For example, Muskalin is a seven-headed dragon described in Buddhist scripture as having protected Buddha when he was meditating in the rain. Those who are possessed by dragons follow a wide array of behavior patterns as Bertrand explains:

[Sometimes a medium] may . . . produce hissing sounds to signal small wild dragons crawling around. . . . The small dragons possess their [medium] in a very violent manner. [Mediums] have great difficulty coming out of their trance when possessed by these small dragons. In fact, the [observer sometimes] has to wake the [medium] up by slapping him slightly or giving him perfume. In contrast to this, the actions of the big dragons, such as Neang Neak . . . are more controlled. They are quite often dressed like [dragon] princesses and they rarely roll on the ground. Neang Neak . . . is jealous, authoritative, and prone to outbursts of anger. [18]

Mediums possessed by animals also emulate the characteristics of the *boramey*. For example, those who are monkeys wear monkey masks, climb on furniture, or swing from branches. The tiger is always roaring, restless and aggressive, and ready to fight. Similar situations exist for crocodiles, white elephants, and the white horse said to have been ridden by Buddha.

Perhaps the most unusual *boramey* are the child spirits. When possessed by these children, mediums use infantile language, play with toys, and perform childish antics to evoke laughter from observers. Each child *boramey* has its own characteristics that distinguish it from others. For example there is "dishonest child," "turbulent child," and "wandering child." In addition to eliciting laughs, these spirits subtly mock childish behavior when seen in adults.

Disease, Accidents, or Bad Luck

Boramey possession is not always voluntary. Many times, a person who suffers disease, an accident, or another episode of bad luck is diagnosed as having a *boramey* possessing him or her. The afflicted can learn about the *boramey* by consulting with a special healer, called an *upachea,* who can name the spirit by observing the patient. This, too, is explained by Bertrand:

> The name given to the boramey is closely related to the behavior of the patient during the treatment sessions. For example, a subject who trembles frequently is called Hong Mea (Golden Stork). In a traditional story, this bird is captured and put into a cage because of its golden feathers, and it trembled when its protective feathers were plucked away. The [medium] of the boramey Tep Macha (Divine Fish) makes movements as if he were swimming.
>
> There are other cases where the [possessed] becomes seriously ill, falls unconscious, and dreams. After waking up, the [patient] claims to have crossed to another world that has an extraordinary landscape and says that the arrival of the boramey as well as its identity had been revealed. [19]

Once the *boramey* is identified, it is possible for the patient to harness its power and reverse his or her problems. In doing so, the possession becomes a positive experience.

Although the *boramey* sect has existed for centuries, it experienced a strong resurgence during Cambodia's exceptionally tragic recent history. Beginning in 1975 a genocidal leader named Pol Pot took control of the country and indiscriminately slaughtered millions of people. While the *boramey* sect predates this tragedy by centuries, the sect gained strength during those dark times even though it was banned by Pol Pot. The mediums claim that the spirits brought them food to keep

Dialogues with the Dead

Throughout the world, various peoples believe that their minds and bodies can be controlled by spirits. Among the Sora people of India, female shamans send their souls to the underworld so that they may give voice to the dead. Piers Vitebsky explains in "Dialogues with the Dead," an article from *Natural History* magazine:

Almost every day among the Sora, a jungle tribe in eastern India, the living conduct dialogues with the dead. A shaman, usually a woman, serves as an intermediary between the two worlds. During a trance, her soul is said to climb down terrifying precipices to the underworld, leaving her body for the dead to use as their vehicle for communication. One by one the spirits speak through her mouth. Mourners crowd around the shaman, arguing vehemently with the dead, laughing at their jokes, or weeping at their accusations.

To prepare her for the important position of intermediary . . . [the shaman] marries a helper spirit, bears spirit children, and makes a second home in the underworld, which she visits every time she dreams or goes into a trance. . . .

According to Sora thinking, death is not the end of existence, but merely another phase. After death one becomes a powerful spirit with contradictory motives. On the one hand, the dead nourish their living descendants by infusing their growing crops with their own "soul force." In aggressive moods, however, they may "eat" their relatives' souls and cause in them the same illness to which the deceased succumbed. . . .

Sora shamans appear to heal . . . by helping the bereaved to manage painful and guilty memories about the dead. Healing is thought to occur only through dialogue. . . . While the shaman goes on her soul journey to the underworld, the bereaved or ailing client also makes an inner journey of discovery. The mourners heal themselves by exploring and modifying the deceased's pain and hostility.

them from starving. They were also said to have taken possession of policemen in order to prevent them from arresting the mediums. As Bertrand explains: "These beliefs about the boramey seem to reflect a denial of the oppressive political power the people experienced and resulted in attributing even more power to the boramey."[20]

Like the loa of Haiti, the *boramey* of Cambodia offer satisfaction, comfort, and knowledge to people whose lives are often grief stricken and short. By communing with ancient kings, dragons, and disciples of Buddha himself, the mediums and their followers can relive a mythical time of beauty and joy. Perhaps these spirits actually do travel through time to bring their wisdom to the people of today. Or they might be elaborate constructs of religious rapture. Whatever the case, they provide comfort, bliss, and unity to believers. And that has long been the traditional role of religion in human societies throughout history.

Possessed by Poltergeists

Possession experiences that involve divination and healing are said to provide positive benefits to mediums and bystanders. There are other types of possession, however, that can wreak havoc and destruction. These allegedly occur when malicious spirits of the dead, called poltergeists, possess innocent victims.

Poltergeists are defined literally as noisy spirits, from the German words *polter*, or "noisy," and *geist*, "spirit." The term was first popularized in the sixteenth century by religious reformer Martin Luther, who was expressing the common belief that certain unsettling events were caused by rambunctious ghosts or other devil-like creatures who either acted alone or worked through possession of innocent victims.

Confused Ghosts

Poltergeists can create mischief by taking control of the mind, body, and soul of a person, known as an "agent." Of the thousands of recorded cases of poltergeist disturbances, researchers estimate that in 99 percent of the cases, agents are most often adolescents, with a majority of them females under the age of twenty. Some may be suffering from psychological disorders such as intensely repressed rage or unhealthy sexual anxiety. Others may be emotionally or physically weak and vulnerable to possession. Those who believe that they are experiencing this poltergeistic possession are often troubled by severe headaches, insomnia, buzzing in the ears, hallucinations, and even insanity.

These symptoms are not at all imaginary; it is their source that is controversial.

Poltergeist possession has been attributed to confused ghosts that do not realize that they are dead and so try to return to living bodies. Although there is little agreement on how poltergeists choose their agents, French spiritualist Allan Kardec tried to find an answer in 1855. Kardec gathered several mediums together for a séance, or a meeting in which a group of people gather around a table in a dark room to call up spirits of the dead. When one such spirit allegedly arrived, Kardec asked it about possession and it replied: "A spirit does not enter a body as you enter a house. He assimilates himself to an incarnate [human being] who has the same defects and the same qualities as himself, in order that they may act conjointly [together]."[21]

Kardec then asked how poltergeists overpower and subjugate agents. The spirit replied that the agent must cooperate either out of weakness, ignorance, or free will. When the spir-

Nineteenth-century spiritualist Allan Kardec held a séance like the one depicted here to discover the cause of possession.

Throwing Stones

When a poltergeist possesses an agent, unexplainable activities may ensue. These episodes are said to be the result of the poltergeist focusing on an agent who feels distress, pain, or fear. By using the agent's psychokinesis, or PK, energy, the poltergeist can create mischief. One such case, documented by unnamed researchers in the 1990s, was described by William G. Roll and Michael A. Persinger in *Hauntings and Poltergeists,* edited by James Houran and Rense Lange:

> In the village of Druten, Holland, sand, stone and clods of earth rained down on a family of Turkish immigrants when Çetin, their 15-year-old son, was near. When the family complained to the police, the officers assumed childish pranks were responsible. Their opinion changed when a female officer had sand thrown in her face while watching Çetin, and a male officer had the same experience when the boy was standing with his hands in his pockets. Later that day, after the first officer had driven Çetin to the home of a relative, sand hit her forcefully on the head while Çetin was still in the car, with the doors locked and the windows shut. The incidents seemed to avoid the researchers [that accompanied the boy to study the phenomena]. . . .
>
> The missiles were mostly directed at Çetin's stepmother and stepsister. This was consistent with the researchers' opinion that Çetin felt they had supplanted him in his father's affection. They noted that stoning is a form of punishment in Islam. . . . The [researchers] found the case to conform to the view that poltergeists are a [supernatural] manifestation . . . [brought out by hurtful] relations.

itualist asked if a victim can be freed through the incantations, commands, and prayers of an exorcism, the spirit answered derisively and said: "No; when bad spirits see any one seriously endeavouring to act upon them by such means, they laugh at him, and persist in their obsession."[22]

Manifestations of Poltergeists

Whether or not Kardec's spirit was correct, it is commonly believed that when a poltergeist does take possession of a victim, havoc ensues. Poltergeist manifestations can include a wide variety of unexplainable phenomena. One of the most common events is a shower of stone, dirt, and sand. Numerous examples have been recorded of rocks and dirt flying at people in enclosed areas such as small rooms and moving automobiles. These objects can sometimes fly in slow motion or take odd trajectories in flight. Similar manifestations can be seen when poltergeist possession results in spontaneous floods, rainstorms, or strong gusts of wind.

Mysterious odors are also said to indicate the presence of a poltergeist. These odors may appear and disappear rapidly and smell as sweet as flowers or as foul and repugnant as human waste. Similarly, odd stains and human excrement can appear on walls and floors when an agent is nearby.

Unexplainable fires in the presence of agents are also common events. Many times these fires are insignificant, such as easily extinguishable flaming matches appearing out of thin air. On occasion they can be more severe, with houses mysteriously combusting and killing the residents. Other fires are simply bizarre, such as the case of Lilly White, a teenage West Indian girl on the Caribbean island of Antigua in the Bahamas. In a 1929 story in the *New York Times,* it was reported that White glowed with a flame that seemed to hover a few inches from her skin. The fire apparently caused her no harm.

Speaking Through an Agent

Probably the most common indicators of poltergeistic activity are unusual sounds such as rapping, pounding, and scratching. Such sounds can resemble furniture moving, thunder crashing, guns firing, rats moving within the walls, repetitive tapping, and violent blows that can shake a house. These may take place in the presence of an agent or be emitted from his or her mouth. For example, agents have said to make whispers, whistles, moans, sobs, shrieks, and evil-sounding guttural voices.

One such unfortunate victim was eleven-year-old Janet Harper of Enfield, England. In 1977 Janet lived with her divorced mother, two brothers, and a sister when a series of poltergeistic activities commenced, each more violent than the last. At first the phenomena resembled what is said to be a typical benevolent poltergeist haunting—chairs moved slightly and loud knocking noises were heard. As happens in many alleged poltergeist cases, the activities increased in violence and intensity. Children's toys such as marbles and building bricks began flying through the air as if launched by a powerful slingshot. On one occasion, a marble picked up by a Harper child was burning hot. These events never happened when Janet was not in the room.

One night when the Harpers' furniture was flying about, psychic investigator Guy Playfair was called. He tried tying a chair to the leg of Janet's bed with several strands of wire, but the wire simply snapped as the chair crashed over sideways and the bed jumped across the room. The poltergeist must have had a sense of humor, because moments later one of Janet's books flew off the shelf, missing Playfair's head by inches. When the book landed upright on the floor, witnesses could read the title, *Fun and Games for Children*.

Janet Harper (left) poses with her family at home. Several poltergeists possessed Janet in the 1970s.

As the poltergeist continued its mischief, a medium named Annie Shaw was brought to the Harper home. After going into a trance, Shaw uttered some guttural phrases, which she said were from ghosts. She then announced that several poltergeists had taken possession of Janet and were using her energy to manifest themselves. After the medium left, the activity slowed for a few weeks, then resumed at a rapid pace with furniture flying, beds shaking, and pools of water appearing on the floor. Janet often reported sensations of being bitten, pinched, and slapped. Playfair recorded four hundred such incidents in a few weeks. The danger increased as an iron fireplace screen sailed across the living room, missing Janet's brother by inches. The next night a one-hundred-pound gas heater was ripped from the wall where it was cemented.

"I Want Some Jazz Music"

Playfair tried to communicate with the poltergeists. When he asked them, "Don't you realize you're dead?" Janet's bedroom erupted violently with every toy, book, article of clothing, and piece of furniture crashing about the room. The poltergeist soon began tossing Janet about as if she were a rag doll, as widely read researcher into paranormal phenomena Colin Wilson explains:

> By now it was very clear that Janet was the poltergeist's main target. She was often thrown out of bed seven or eight times before she succeeded in getting to sleep. When she fell asleep, she twitched and moaned; Playfair began to feel increasingly that she was possessed. . . .
>
> The following night, Janet had more convulsions, and wandered around, talking aloud. "Where's Gober? He'll kill you." . . . Soon after this, Janet began producing drawings, in a state of semi-trance; one of them showed a woman with blood pouring out of her throat, with the name "Watson" written underneath. Other drawings continued this theme of blood, knives, and death. [23]

Good and Bad Spirits

In *The Spirits' Book*, written in 1857, Allan Kardec defined the actions and motives of both good spirits and bad spirits such as poltergeists:

> Spirits are attracted by their sympathy with the moral quality of the parties by whom they are [entwined]. Spirits of superior elevation take pleasure in meetings of a serious character, animated by the love of goodness and the sincere desire of instruction and improvement. Their presence repels the spirits of inferior degree [such as poltergeists] who find, on the contrary, free access and freedom of action among persons of frivolous disposition . . . wherever evil instincts are to be met with. So far from obtaining from spirits . . . either good advice or useful information, nothing is to be expected from them but trifling, lies, ill-natured tricks, or humbugging. . . .
>
> It is easy to distinguish between good and bad spirits. The language of spirits of superior elevation is constantly dignified, noble, characterised by the highest morality, free from every trace of earthly passion; their counsels breathe the purest wisdom, and always have our improvement and the good of mankind for their aim. The communications of spirits of lower degree, on the contrary, are full of discrepancies, and their language is often commonplace, and even coarse. If they sometimes say things that are good and true, they more often make false and absurd statements, prompted by ignorance or malice. They play upon the credulity of those who interrogate them, amusing themselves by flattering their vanity, and fooling them with false hopes.

Janet eventually began to emit strange growling voices while in a trancelike state. She channeled one entity, who could not speak without cursing. It said its name was Joe Watson. Another was named Bill, who informed a medium that he once had a dog named Gober the Ghost. When asked why he was shaking Janet's bed, he said he was sleeping there first. When asked where he came from, he said, "From the graveyard." When asked why he didn't go "up there," he said in a jerky voice: "I'm not in heaven, man . . . I am Bill Haylock and . . . I am seventy-two years old and I have come here to see my family but they are not here now. . . . You . . . old bitch, shut up. I want some jazz music now go and get me some or else I'll go barmy [insane]."[24] This odd voice, which was taped, came out of the young girl one word at a time in a tone that sounded like a very old man.

After many more months, this bizarre possession ceased for reasons unknown. Playfair later stated that the number of entities possessing Janet was "half the local graveyard at one time or another."[25] In addition to Joe Watson and Bill Haylock, the young girl might have been haunted by up to a dozen different poltergeists. To explain why this happened, Playfair stated:

> When Mr. and Mrs. Harper were divorced, an atmosphere of tension built up among the children and their mother, just at a time when [Janet] was approaching

physical maturity. [She was very energetic but she] could not use up the tremendous energy [she] was generating. So a number of entities came in and helped themselves to it.[26]

Whatever the cause, Harper's case was similar to other poltergeist possessions in that it started and stopped abruptly. This is different than "normal" ghostly activity that can continue for decades or even centuries.

Energy Leakage

Playfair believed that the Harper possession was caused by psychokinesis, or PK, energy manifested by Janet. The term *psychokinesis* is derived from the Greek words *psyche* meaning "life" or "soul," and *kinein* meaning "to move." With PK energy, agents such as Janet can allegedly utilize mental powers to bend spoons, make dishes fly through the air, create foul odors, make hideous scratching sounds within the walls of a house, or provoke other poltergeistic phenomena.

In *Poltergeist: A Study in Destructive Haunting,* Colin Wilson explains why poltergeists work through adolescents to generate such pranks:

Physical changes that occur during puberty cause a "leakage" of [PK] energy that can be used by a poltergeist; this energy is probably some kind of nerve-force. When the physical adjustments of puberty have been made, the leak stops, and the poltergeist can no longer manifest itself.[27]

Such energy leaks are not confined only to adolescents, however. They also seem to be present where a child has experienced some sort of trauma. In one case documented in 1941 in Cornwall, England, various odd disturbances were observed around an unnamed nine-year-old boy. The poltergeist activity began soon after the child's baby sister died. At first the boy performed acts that were easily explained. For example, he was seen turning over a living room table. When confronted, however, he claimed that some unseen power forced him to rise from his chair and tip over the table.

The child was put into the living room alone where he could be observed by his mother, the local clergyman, and others peering through window shades. The observers saw the boy throw a tin can across the room. Inexplicably, the can quickly rose off the ground into the air and flew back into the boy's hand. After seeing this, his astonished mother took him into the kitchen and tied his hands behind his back with a belt. As witnesses watched through a crack in the door, the pots, pans, and kitchen chairs began jumping and bouncing around the room.

The boy was sent away from his home, and the poltergeist activities stopped. When he returned, it continued for a short

A young man surveys the damage done to his room by a poltergeist. Such spirits often use energy "leaked" from troubled psyches.

time and then permanently ceased. The episode is explained by Wilson, who writes, "It seems clear that the shock of his sister's death caused the kind of 'energy leak' that gave the poltergeist its energy. But it was also able to force the boy to throw things."[28] Researchers speculate that the type of pain and fear the boy experienced from his sister's death might be similar to the suffering felt by the poltergeist when it first became a ghost.

The Amherst Mystery

The Cornwall incident was a common type of poltergeist episode that lasted only a short time. Some puzzling cases, however, torment the victim for many months with little relief. One such case attracted widespread attention in Amherst, Nova Scotia, Canada, beginning in September 1878.

The episode concerned Daniel Teed and his wife, Olive Cox Teed, and Mrs. Teed's niece, nineteen-year-old Esther Cox. The trouble started when Esther Cox was traumatized by Bob MacNeal, a local shoemaker who attempted to rape her. Although Cox escaped with minor injuries, her trauma apparently made her an agent for a poltergeist, and a sequence of inexplicable events followed the assault.

The first events were minor: small fires, mysterious voices, and rapping noises heard by the residents of the Teed home on Church Street. The disturbances soon began to escalate and further traumatize the already fearful Cox. One night, soon after she went to bed, the young woman woke up screaming. Her hair was standing on end, her face was flushed bright red, and her body had inflated like a toy balloon. As the Teeds rushed to her side, a loud clap of thunder was heard and witnesses ran from the room to investigate. When they returned, Cox was back to her normal size. Two days later, another bizarre swelling episode coincided with the sheets and pillows flying off Cox's bed several times. The next day a doctor came to examine Cox. While he was there, her pillow inflated and deflated several times and a sheet flew off the bed. Cox, meanwhile, complained of an electric tingling running through her body. The doctor sedated her with morphine. As she fell asleep, a series of loud crashes and bangs was heard on the roof.

Electrified by Several Spirits

The next several months were pure anguish for Cox as the activities continued. In her presence, buckets of water appeared to boil as if they were on a stove. Lit matches appeared out of thin air over her bed and started the sheets and blankets on fire. When a barrel of wood shavings spontaneously combusted in the basement and was difficult to extinguish, the Teeds sent the troubled young woman away.

Cox went to work for a neighbor named John White, who owned a restaurant. Unfortunately, the poltergeist possession continued to create problems where Cox worked in the kitchen. On one occasion the oven door flew off its hinges and crashed to the floor. Another time metal forks, knives, and spoons flew across the room and stuck to Cox as if she were a magnet. When she tried to clean utensils, items she held in her lap became too hot to touch. Such incidents led witnesses to believe that she was somehow "electrified." Her doctor gave her glass shoes to wear, thinking they might shield her from some sort of magnetic charge he incorrectly believed was emitted from the earth. When she wore the shoes, however, Cox was inexplicably stricken with nosebleeds and severe headaches.

Hoping to find an answer to her problem, the young woman consulted spiritualists. During one séance, Cox practiced automatic writing and allegedly communicated a message from a ghost named Maggie Fisher. The ghost said that it had attended the same school as Cox but had died around 1867, before graduating. Cox had not known Fisher personally, but had heard of her at school. Soon other ghosts came forth including Bob Nickle who, like the rapist Bob MacNeal, was a shoemaker. Other ghosts included Peter Teed, John Nickle, and Eliza MacNeal. Their motives for torturing Cox remained unclear.

Some remained skeptical that Cox could be possessed by so many poltergeists at once. Despite the disbelief, Cox became a celebrity as townspeople came to visit her to witness the disturbances. In June 1879 a magician named Walter Hubbell visited Amherst to investigate the now-famous Cox. He later wrote that he was quickly shown that the activities were not fraudulent. Within minutes of his arrival, an umbrella flew through the air, a carving knife dropped at his feet, and a chair sailed across the room and hit him so hard he fell to the ground. After that, whenever he walked into a room, the chairs danced. Cox informed Hubbell that her poltergeists did not like him.

Located in Amherst, Nova Scotia, this house was the scene of Elizabeth Cox's poltergeist possession in 1878–1879.

Hoping to make some money from the poltergeistic possession, Hubbell and Cox went on a tour of local theaters in June 1879. The mischievous ghosts refused to cooperate, however, and skeptical audiences angrily demanded their money back when no unusual phenomena ensued.

Back in Amherst, the manifestations continued until Cox went to work as a housekeeper for a local farmer named Arthur Davison. Davison did not believe in poltergeists and when his barn burned to the ground, he accused Cox of arson. She was convicted and sent to prison for four months. Public outcry forced the courts to look again at the evidence and free her after only one month. After this experience, as in most other recorded poltergeistic activity, the symptoms seemed to simply go away, and Cox was not troubled by poltergeist events again.

A Poltergeist in a Mongoose

While poltergeists occasionally possess human beings, an odd case from Great Britain concerns a poltergeist possession of an animal. The episode occurred at the isolated farmhouse of the Irving family near Cashen's Gap on the Isle of Man. The witnesses were James Irving, his wife, and their thirteen-year-old daughter, Voirrey.

In September 1931, the Irvings began to hear strange noises emanating from their attic. They heard barking, growling, hissing, spitting, and a sound that resembled baby gurgling. While attempting to communicate with the noisemaker, Voirrey found that it would repeat nursery rhymes she recited. Finally, the animal came out of hiding. It was allegedly a small furry mongoose that introduced himself as Gef. The mongoose claimed to have been born June 7, 1852, in Delhi, India, but never explained how he came to live on the small island in the Irish Sea. Although Mr. Irving only saw glimpses of Gef, Voirrey often saw it.

Gef created a great deal of mischief with poltergeist activities. Objects flew through the air and shrieking noises erupted from behind the walls. Oddly, Gef allegedly spoke Russian, sang hymns in Spanish, and could read minds. It also killed rabbits by strangling them. When paranormal investigators traveled to Cashen's Gap to examine the phenomenon, Gef disappeared until they left.

The strange case of Gef continued until 1937, when the Irvings abruptly sold their farm and disappeared. While some believe the family had perpetrated a hoax, investigators said they seemed sincere. And they doubted anyone would make up the unlikely idea of a talking mongoose simply to get attention. Instead, the poltergeist possession was attributed to Voirrey, since such activity is often traced to adolescent girls. Why—or whether—the spirit-possessed mongoose really existed remains unanswered.

After Cox died in 1912, Hubbell published a book, *The Great Amherst Mystery*, that detailed her story. It included affidavits from sixteen Amherst residents who had witnessed the hauntings. Although the book sold well, some believed that Hubbell had embellished the story and that is was more fiction than fact. Few could explain, however, why Cox was prone to inflate to twice her normal size, why objects stuck to her body, or how fires started in her presence.

Poltergeists or Unhealthy Anger?

While many believed that poltergeists are malevolent ghosts acting through agents, others have explanations that are more natural than supernatural. In the 1960s, researcher William Roll, director of the Psychical Research Center in Durham, North Carolina, studied more than 115 written reports of poltergeists recorded in more than one hundred countries during the previous four hundred years. Roll found that while PK energy may have been responsible for inexplicable poltergeistic activity, there were no ghosts involved.

Instead, Roll believed, it was a way for the agents to express rage toward their families. This anger may have resulted from a punishment, feelings of unfair treatment, or a traumatic experience. By blaming their behavior on a supernatural source, agents were able to act in ways that were completely unacceptable. However, instead of being punished for their behavior, they received a great deal of attention and sympathy from their worried family members. While many agents claimed to be unaware of the disturbances they were causing, when told about them later they recorded feelings of happiness over the troubles they were causing, perhaps thinking of their mischief in terms of revenge.

The question as to whether poltergeists are malicious ghosts or mischievous mortals remains unanswered. The fears of those who witness poltergeistic phenomena, however, are very real. As real, perhaps, as the furniture flying through the air, propelled by some mysterious force.

Chapter 4

Diabolical Possession

O ver the centuries, people have recorded acts of possession by a wide variety of spirits, ghosts, and poltergeists. Of all the claims perhaps none is regarded as more terrifying than that of diabolical possession.

When someone is possessed by the devil, Satan is said to control and torment that person. This makes the situation different than other types of possession for several reasons. While poltergeists might create mischief for a short period of time before disappearing, the devil is said to lay claim to the victim's very soul. And while the poltergeist almost always leaves, satanic possession can last a lifetime and even be handed down from one generation to the next.

Possession by Satan has strong religious overtones and is closely associated with some Christian beliefs. Because diabolical possession is mentioned in the New Testament, those who believe that the Bible is the literal truth have no doubts that possession is real. Over the centuries, however, some religious scholars have tried to diminish its importance, as theologian T.K. Oesterreich writes in *Possession Demoniacal & Other:*

> [Actions] which would formerly have been considered as demoniacal are now regarded as "natural," and there is a general weakening in the conviction that there exist demons and spirits of the dead who may be a source of danger to the living. Writing on practical theology

shows a unanimous tendency to warn the reader that possession should not be too readily admitted. A case of possession is always a matter for the higher ecclesiastical authorities; it is, in a word, an event which has become very rare.[29]

Despite such reassurances, the belief in diabolical possession remains quite strong among millions of people today. The concept was popularized in 1973 when the movie *The Exorcist* played to packed movie houses. In this horror classic, a mother believes that her twelve-year-old daughter is possessed by an evil spirit and calls in two priests to exorcise the demon. The

Reports of demonic possessions rose markedly after the 1973 release of the movie The Exorcist, *from which this scene is taken.*

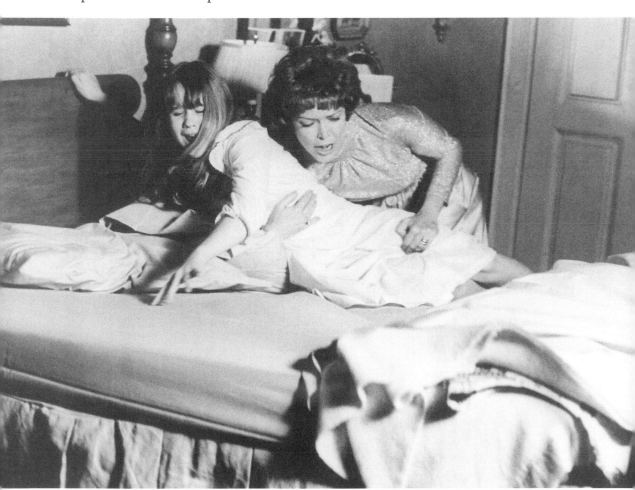

girl exhibits classic symptoms of possession as she spews obscenities and vomit and her head rotates in circles on her neck.

Probably because *The Exorcist* went on to become one of the top-grossing films in history, by the mid-seventies religious institutions recorded a huge increase in the number of people reporting demonic possession. With the public hungry to find out more, dozens of books were written on the subject. Although it became a sort of fad, the question as to whether or not demonic possession is an actual physical or mental condition remains to be answered. There are, however, thousands of people who say they are, or have been, possessed by the devil. They have exhibited similar types of behavior and have reported their conditions as a warning to others.

Symptoms of Possession

People in the throes of diabolical possession often exhibit extreme and frightening symptoms. They may show signs of mental illness or display obvious repugnance when shown religious symbols such as a cross or the Bible. Sometimes bizarre phenomena may ensue that is also typically associated with poltergeists. For example, paint can peel, strange noises may be heard in the walls, glasses of water can appear to boil, and objects such as dishes and furniture can float off the ground or dance around the room. Possession can also affect the immediate environment in odd ways—sudden drops in temperature and the acrid stench of foul odors are commonly described by witnesses.

An example of a woman, known only as "U," exhibited what are considered classic symptoms of possession. Her condition was described in 1834 by German author Justinus Kerner:

> In this state the eyes were tightly shut, the face grimacing, often excessively and horribly changed, the voice [of the demon speaking through her] repugnant, full of shrill cries, deep groans, coarse words; the speech expressing the joy of inflicting hurt or cursing God and the universe, addressing terrible threats now to the [ob-

servers], now to the patient herself. . . . The most dreadful thing was the way in which she raged . . . threatening all those who approached, insulting and abusing them in the vilest terms; her body bent backwards like a bow was flung out of the chair and writhed upon the ground, then lay there stretched out at full length, stiff and cold, assuming the very appearance of death. If in spite of her resistance anyone succeeded in administering [food] to the patient she at once manifested a violent movement to vomit up again what had been forced upon her. This occurred each time with diabolic howlings and a terrible panting, alternating with satanic bursts of laughter in a piercing falsetto.[30]

Other symptoms of diabolical possession include bizarre swellings and distortions of the body. Also seen in poltergeist possession, these swellings can be quite pronounced and beyond any treatment. This was the case in the 1860s of the alleged demonic possession of Theobald Illfurth, a young German boy. Author Peter Sutter describes the situation:

At times, [Theobald's] body became swollen in the most unnatural manner; his breath whistled and his chest moved in and out like a bellows. A local member of the gendarmerie [police force], Herr Werner, tried with all his might to halt these movements by pressing against the boy's chest and belly. He was joined by a second man, then by a third and a fourth. The policeman then yielded his place to a miller, an unusually strong man. All four now pressed against the possessed boy's body until the [bed frame] creaked, but without success. Fearing that they might injure the boy's internal organs, Werner urged them to stop their efforts. But the boy shouted, "Don't worry about it. . . . You might just as well call a few more men, and you'll still be unable to accomplish anything."[31]

Other swellings may be more localized. In a case from Germany in 1605, the victim was said to have a huge swelling on her head the size of an apple. Other physical manifestations of possession might include partial paralysis and loss of sight, hearing, or speech.

Letters Burned into Skin

Some of the most painful indications of diabolical possession occur on the skin. It is said that if a priest sprinkles holy water on a person whom the devil possesses, the liquid will leave burn marks. This may also be true if a cross is placed upon the victim. These burns are said to be quite severe and can take weeks to heal. Equally peculiar are letters that appear to be branded into the victim's skin, said to spell out words such as *evil* or the devil's name. In *Possessed by Satan*, Adolf Rodewyk describes this eerie phenomenon:

> We have records of cases in which such skin writings developed within the sight of others present. These writings did not fade for weeks or months, so that fraud or artificial methods can be excluded. Those who observed these phenomena regarded them as surprising and odd, while the possessed experienced them as causes of intense pain, much as if burns or acid-caused injuries affected considerable portions of the skin. [32]

Other skin abrasions are varied and strange. The Illfurth boy was alleged to have hoof prints on his skin where he said the devil had kicked him. Others show marks as if they were flogged with sticks, straps, and whips.

Naturally, manifestations of Satan can drive the possessed to the brink of insanity. Those who experience such symptoms often begin to show signs of mental illness, experiencing hallucinations, hysteria, and uncontrollable weeping. Some try to harm themselves, hoping to drive the devil from their bodies. A German girl known only as Magda used a razor to cut herself more than ninety times. In a diabolical twist, Satan al-

Developing Strange Tastes

Oftentimes those said to be possessed by the devil exhibit odd eating habits. The victim stops eating but does not lose weight, or eats voraciously without weight gain. In *Possessed by Satan,* Jesuit scholar Adolf Rodewyk discusses food intake among the possessed:

> We often observe that the possessed . . . [avoid] food that has been sprinkled with holy water. . . . But quite aside from this, there is a pattern whereby the possessed even leave untouched food of which they are quite fond and which they had anticipated with pleasure; often they refuse the food, saying, "The Devil won't let me eat it." No amount of encouragement will make them change their minds. The food may even cause a revolting taste in their mouths, which is another way of keeping them from eating properly. Contrariwise, the possessed may find themselves forced to swallow revolting things. [Fifth-century bishop, Saint] Paulinus of Nola speaks of a man who tore chickens to pieces and gulped them down, feathers and all; he also took the bones of dead animals away from dogs and gnawed on them. Even such completely indigestible things as iron or coal are swallowed. . . . Such things are often very taxing to the possessed men and women, particularly when the Devil permits them to comprehend what they are forced to do; but he so paralyzes their will that they cannot help themselves. Some of these items are later vomited up, but much is, quite remarkably, digested.

legedly told Magda days or weeks ahead of time when he would force her to injure herself. This caused her great anxiety as she fearfully tried to live her life while anticipating the forthcoming pain. Although her parents tried to remove all sharp objects from the home, Magda always managed to find a way to slash herself.

Such fears force some victims to consider suicide, although demoniacs rarely kill themselves. As Rodewyk writes: "Although the Devil may drive the possessed to the brink of desperation, he has to guard against the final act. He is concerned with suffering and torture [and so he wants his victims to live so that he can prolong their misery]."[33]

Why the Devil Moves In

Theologians have long debated precisely how the devil chooses his victims. While some believe that victims are usually innocent, others believe that some have asked or allowed the devil to possess them. Those who ascribe to the blameless victim theory say that the devil looks for people who are emotionally wounded. This weakness allows the devil to take control. When this happens, some say, doctors trying to treat the victim might not understand that Satan is behind the problem. This is especially true for possessed children, as Lutheran minister, psychologist, and professional exorcist Ken Olson writes:

Exorcists try to free a possessed young man. Just how demons choose their victims is debated.

Deeply traumatic experiences can open children to tormenting spirits of fear, rage, or bitterness. . . . Because the emotions are so strong, the focus of attention is on

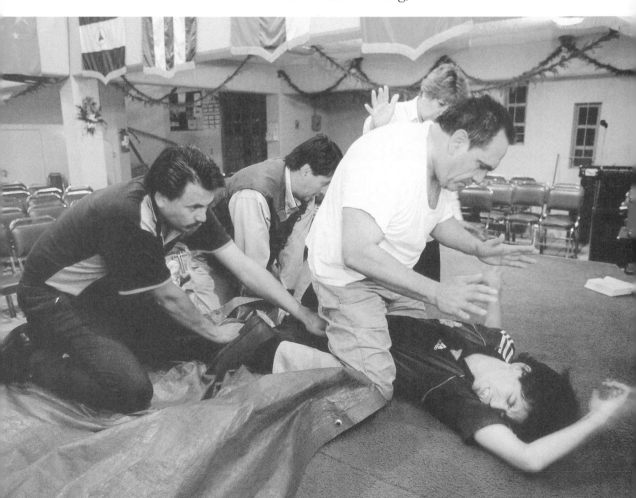

these intense feelings, and consequently, the presence of a demonic entity within can go undetected. Demons can hide behind these feelings, exercising influence and control and empowering self-destructive behaviors.[34]

Afflicted children might also allegedly become victims because their relatives are sinners, wicked people who are said to ignore religion and biblical teachings. In these cases, the child is alleged to be cursed because of the deeds of his or her parents, grandparents, or great-grandparents. Some religious thinkers even ascribe to the theory that the curse can go back generations and might be handed down from father to son or mother to daughter for hundreds of years. When this happens, a person may ostensibly be chosen by the devil even before birth.

Making a Pact with the Devil

Blaming the victim is common among those who believe in diabolical possession. It is often thought that the possessed brought the curse upon him- or herself through various actions and behaviors.

One of the most common concepts, used in countless stories over the centuries, is that the possessed "sold his soul to the devil" in exchange for money, success, and power. In such cases, the devil promises to fulfill the wishes of the victim if he or she signs—sometimes in blood—a legal contract promising the soul in exchange for the wishes. Olson, who has dealt with people who have claimed to have made such a pact, writes: "One woman told me that in a satanic ritual she received a very strong demon of power to rule her. When this demon entered her, she said, it was like being filled with liquid fire and incredible pain."[35]

While most victims of diabolical possession do not explicitly sell their souls, some are offered help by a friendly stranger who is allegedly the devil in disguise. Although the victims might be suspicious, they seem to go along with Satan because they feel he can help them. In *Hostage to the Devil,*

This medieval woodcut depicts a monk making a pact with the devil. Such acts imply that in some cases possession may be voluntary.

former exorcist Malachi Martin details the stories of five people who said they were possessed by the devil. He writes:

> [All] admit in retrospect that they knew . . . that the source of the offered help was neither a human being or any religious source. The source was always vague, always reassuring. It always alienated them from their surroundings and from those nearest to

them. The general feeling was "great things could happen to them," or "new developments could take place" in them, or "special success" would be theirs if they were to "listen" or to "think along these lines." . . . At some point during this earliest stage, there arrives a delicate moment when each person *chooses* to consider the particular *offer* made to him or her. The [victims agree] . . . that they made such a choice, and that they had a sense of violating their consciences when they made it, though at the time in some cases it seemed a fairly minor violation. [36]

While selling one's soul to the devil is a voluntary act, diabolical possession can allegedly overtake people involuntarily if they commit acts the church labels sinful. As Olson writes, "when a sin is repeated, encouraged, and unrepented, it can lead to demonization." [37] According to religious thinkers, such sins can include alcohol, drug, and sexual abuse, as well as violence and other violations of religious teachings. Alcohol abuse is particularly close to possession, as people who are very drunk can exhibit behavior similar to demonization, including foul language, excessive vomiting, cursing religious symbols, and other symptoms.

How the Devil Takes Over

Whatever the catalyst for possession, those who are exposed to demonization are said to open a kind of spiritual doorway that allows Satan to enter their physical body. Once this happens, the devil gains access to their personality and soul. Allowing the devil to take over is always said to be a voluntary act, a decision, however slight, to allow the spirit to gain control. Then, as Martin writes, two more steps allow the devil to gain total control:

> [A] stage of *erroneous judgments* by the possessed in vital matters . . . [followed by] the *voluntary yielding of*

control by the possessed person to a force or presence he clearly feels is alien to himself and as a result of which the possessed loses control of his will, and so his decisions and actions. . . . Once the [final] stage is secure, extended control proceeds and may potentially reach the point of completion—perfect possession. [38]

Martin defines erroneous, or flawed, judgments as victims denying their obligations to God's authority or ignoring or doubting their religious beliefs.

Sometimes the first two steps of the process happen quickly; other times they take place over a matter of years or even decades. Each step can proceed only with the permission, however subtle, of the possessed. And once consent is granted, it is very difficult to retract. In some cases, when victims have thoughts of revoking permission, they are stricken with intense pain, vivid and ghastly nightmares, or other horrors.

Defining the Soul

The belief that each human has a soul that guides his or her actions is nearly universal. While the soul might be common to all humanity, few have been able to accurately define just what it is. In *How About Demons?*, Felicitas D. Goodman uses a modern analogy to describe the function of the soul:

[Those] cleaving to the "soul hypothesis" [say] humans consist of a shell, something like a box, namely, the body, and an ephemeral substance or essence residing within, usually termed the soul. . . .

To clarify some of the ramifications of the soul theory, let us couch it in some seemingly simplistic imagery: for those accepting the soul hypothesis, a human being could be likened to a car with a driver in it. The car is the body, and the driver is the soul. This simile makes it easier for us than any theoretical discussion could to understand what people mean when they talk about the experience of possession. Just as the driver owns the car, so the soul owns the body. The owner of the car drives the vehicle, and it is the soul that activates the body. Now, suppose the driver has a friend who has no car. What might happen? The driver, if he is so inclined, could invite this friend temporarily to take over the wheel and to drive the car. In terms of the soul theory, something of this sort happens in possession.

After the first two phases pass, the possessed makes a final choice—at a single critical moment—to voluntarily yield control to the devil. Martin writes that the victims he knew "felt an eerie 'pressure' to allow 'someone else' to give them directives; and that 'someone else' was 'inside' them in some way or other. The pressure was not physical. . . . Once they yielded they started to receive 'instructions'—ready-made judgments . . . arose in them, even words on their lips and actions in their limbs." [39]

Once Satan has banished a victim's free will, he takes immediate measures to protect his position. Any people, places, or things that might challenge his power are avoided. This might include friends, families, priests, religious symbols, and the church. Even as behavior changes dramatically, the sufferer can only passively observe, as if a stranger within his or her own body. A victim of possession named Carl states, "I would think and say and do things without being able to say why and without any prior reason or motivation." [40]

Banishing Satan

When the devil allegedly gains total control over a victim, outsiders might not even realize it. The possessed person might simply avoid all human contact. In such situations, attempts by exorcists to banish the devil will not succeed. Just as it takes the victim's consent for the devil to enter, the victim must give permission for an exorcism to work. This can happen when some small part of a person's soul remains untainted by the devil, or some speck of doubt remains. At such times the possessed can revolt against Satan and a battle over control ensues with the devil using all his supernatural powers of evil to fight expulsion.

Ironically, it is often the battle to expel Satan that brings on the terrifying symptoms associated with possession. As the devil struggles to retain his position, he forces the victim to vomit, foam at the mouth, shout obscenities, and so on. This is the time when the exorcist can do the most good, helping the victim to drive off the devil.

A Case Study of Diabolical Possession

The job of the exorcist was made famous in the film *The Exorcist* in 1973. The movie, however, was adapted from William Peter Blatty's best-selling 1971 novel of the same name. The book was based on the story of allegedly real events that took place near Washington, D.C., in 1949.

Blatty wrote the book about a boy he saw mentioned in an August 20, 1949, *Washington Post* article entitled "Priest Frees Mt. Rainier Boy Reported Held in Devil's Grip."[41] (The boy actually lived in Cottage City, Maryland, a small community just a short distance away from Mt. Rainier. The identity of the town was left out of the article to protect the child's privacy.)

The story began in January 1949 and involved a thirteen-year-old boy named Robbie who lived with his parents and grandmother. Robbie was very close to his aunt, who often visited from St. Louis. The aunt was a medium who allegedly communicated with spirits. She showed Robbie how to use a Ouija board, a fortune-telling device on which people put their hands on a pointer that supposedly spells out answers to questions about the future.

Robbie began using the Ouija board quite a bit leading up to the odd phenomena. At first the family heard scratching in the walls. Exterminators were called, but they found no rats or mice that could have caused the noise. Soon objects around the house began to move by themselves. For example, a table turned over, a chair danced around the room, a vase flew through the air, and a picture of Jesus shook in a frightening manner.

When the aunt died suddenly at the end of January 1949, Robbie claimed to communicate with her using the Ouija board. During this period, Robbie's personality began to change as he became restless and prone to angry outbursts. Robbie's mother took him to Reverend Schulze, a Lutheran minister, who let Robbie move into his house. One night an armchair

in which the boy sat seemingly tilted on its own and tipped over. Robbie's bed was also said to shake and move by itself.

Schulze decided Robbie was possessed by the devil and told the family to contact a Catholic priest, Father Hughes of St. James Catholic Church in Mt. Rainier. During an interview with Robbie in his office, Hughes saw objects moving as the young boy shouted a stream of blasphemous and obscene remarks.

The Exorcist author Peter Blatty, actress Linda Blair, and technical adviser Reverend William O'Malley (right to left) pose at the film's premiere. Real events inspired the book this film was based on.

Howling, Growling, and Shouting

Robbie was admitted to Georgetown Hospital, where Father Hughes began the ritual of exorcism. The boy became violent, spitting, projectile vomiting, and shrieking obscenities. When the priest tied him to the bed with strong rope, Robbie easily broke loose. With seemingly superhuman strength, the boy pulled a metal spring from the bed and slashed Hughes. The wound was so severe it required more than one hundred stitches. After this, however, Robbie calmed down and claimed no memory of the episode. He soon returned home.

Within days Robbie's symptoms of diabolical possession returned. One night Robbie woke up screaming. When his parents came to check on him, they saw the bloody word "Louis" carved into the boy's chest. Thinking of Robbie's dead aunt, they asked if this meant St. Louis. Another gruesome word appeared: "Yes."

The family took Robbie to St. Louis where he was examined by several other priests, who witnessed the same alleged diabolical phenomena as Hughes and Schulze. Furniture shook and moved and the boy yelled curses. Robbie was taken to another hospital and a second exorcism was attempted. During this episode, Robbie took to howling, growling, and shouting. In front of witnesses, more letters supposedly appeared on his chest spelling out "hell" and "devil."

As the exorcists reached a pitched battle with Satan, the devil was expelled from Robbie. The sound of a gunshot was said to be heard throughout the hospital. On April 18, the ordeal was over. Robbie remembered nothing of the diabolical possession.

Raising Doubts About Robbie's Story

While Robbie's story was turned into a best seller, some people doubt that the boy was ever truly possessed by Satan. When Mark Chorvinsky investigated the claims for an article in *Strange Magazine,* he found that most of the events described in the book were based on the diary of Father Bishop, one of several St. Louis exorcists. Bishop simply recorded second- or third-hand accounts of incidents of moving furniture and scratching in the walls. As Chorvinsky writes:

> Bishop does not always make it clear who actually witnessed the events being described—he often fails to mention when the priests are in the room, when they

are absent, and when the information comes second-hand from the boy's mother; the possibility of fraudulent activity is neither considered nor investigated (for example, no control experiment was set up where an individual could observe the boy's actions when no one else was in the room). [42]

There are similar doubts about the bloody letters supposedly etched into Robbie's skin. When Chorvinsky asked a priest who was there if he actually saw blood dripping from the letters, the priest said, it "looked more like lipstick." [43] Further investigation showed that Robbie was a troubled boy who may have staged the entire episode in order to attract attention. As Chorvinsky writes:

There is simply too much evidence that indicates that as a boy he had serious emotional problems stemming

Medical Problems Diagnosed as Possession

People suffer from many medical conditions that were once diagnosed as demonic possession. In *Hostage to the Devil*, Malachi Martin discusses some of these diseases and their symptoms:

[Many] who claim to be possessed or whom others so describe are merely the victims of some mental or physical disease. In reading records from times when medical and psychological science did not exist or were quite undeveloped, it is clear that grave mistakes were made. A victim of disseminated sclerosis, for example, was taken to be possessed because of his spastic jerkings . . . and the shocking agony in the spinal column and joints. Until quite recently, the victim of Tourette's syndrome was

the perfect target for the accusation of "Possessed!": [symptoms of Tourette's syndrome include] torrents of profanities and obscenities, grunts, barks, curses, yelps, snorts, sniffs, tics, foot stomping, facial contortions. [These] all appear suddenly and just as suddenly cease in the subject. Nowadays, Tourette's syndrome responds to drug treatment, and it seems to be a neurological disease involving a chemical abnormality in the brain. Many people suffering from illnesses and diseases well known to us today such as paranoia, Huntington's chorea, dyslexia, Parkinson's disease, or even mere skin diseases (psoriasis, herpes I, for instance), were treated as people "possessed" or at least as "touched" by the Devil.

The demoniac's mother and exorcist helplessly watch her in this scene from The Exorcist. *The film widely popularized possession.*

from his home life. There is not one shred of hard evidence to support the notion of demonic possession. The facts show that he was a spoiled and disturbed only child with a very overprotective mother and a nonresponsive father. To me his behavior was indicative of an outcast youth who desperately wanted out of . . . Junior High School at any cost. He wanted attention and he wanted to leave the area and go to St. Louis. Throwing tantrums was the answer. He began to play

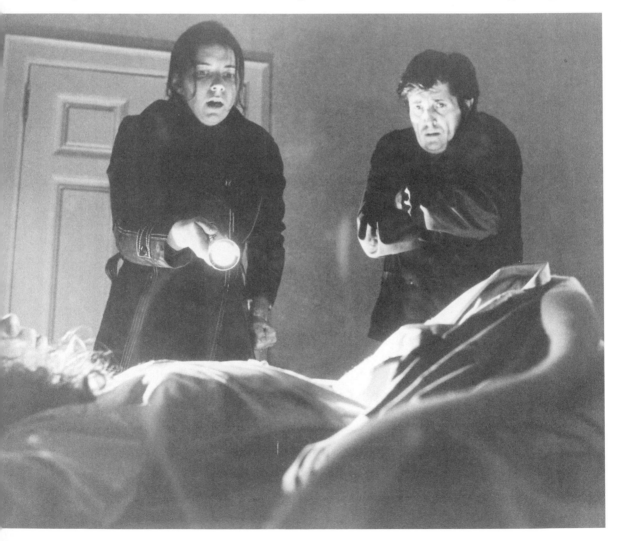

his concocted game. For his efforts he got a collection of priests (who had no previous exorcism experience) who doted over him as he lay strapped to a bed. His response was that of any normal child—he reacted with rage, he wanted out. Without delving into the dynamics of psychosomatic illness, there is no question there was something wrong with [Robbie] prior to January 1949, something that modern-era psychiatry might have best addressed. [Robbie] was not just another normal teenage boy. [44]

Whether or not Robbie was possessed, when his story was fictionalized in *The Exorcist,* the case took the concept of diabolical possession out of obscurity and made it a modern cultural phenomenon. Since the release of the movie, there have been hundreds of "copycat" cases around the world. Some of these cases had serious consequences with those allegedly possessed being battered, abused, and even killed in botched exorcisms. For example, in 1995 Pentecostal ministers in San Francisco beat a woman to death while trying to drive the demons out of her.

With belief in the devil as old as written history, there is little doubt that claims of diabolical possession will continue well into the future. While these assertions may be a matter of religious faith, no one has produced scientific proof that such torments are anything more than the products of overactive imaginations or mental illness. Until such time as researchers develop an accurate test for demonization, it will be up to each individual to decide whether or not it is possible for someone to be possessed by Satan.

Chapter 5

Exorcising the Devil

W hen a person is said to be possessed by the devil, it is often very difficult for friends, family, or the victim to expel the demon. Oftentimes an exorcist is called in to perform a religious rite in which Satan is coaxed, cajoled, or commanded to leave the victim's body and soul.

The idea of exorcism is as old as humanity and has been used in various cultures to drive all manner of evil spirits, ghosts, and demons from the body. Because it was mentioned extensively in the New Testament, the concept of exorcism has been applied primarily by Christians attempting to fight off Satan. Jesus was an exorcist. As Acts 10:38 states, he "went about doing good, and healing all that were oppressed [by] the devil." And as Baker explains, Jesus "made a firm articulation of the tension between God and the devil, and subsequently exorcism and possession became concrete facts of Christianity."[45] But in *Unclean Spirits,* D.P. Walker says he believes that the tales of exorcism were used as much to spread the doctrine of the Church as they were to heal those possessed:

> The exorcisms performed by Christ and the Apostles and disciples were intended, together with other miracles, to establish a new religion; and exorcisms were used in the first few centuries of the Church's life as a weapon against the pagan gods, who regularly appear as possessing devils. But by the Middle Ages the main

purpose of exorcisms, apart of course from curing the demoniac, seems to have been to demonstrate the sanctity of the exorcist. [46]

Whatever the case, thousands of exorcists, most of them men, operate throughout the world today. Many are religious professionals such as priests. Some, however, are self-taught exorcists who, as Baker writes, feel "that they have been possessed by the Holy Spirit and therefore have the gift of [identifying] . . . demons working in other, troubled, people." [47]

The Exorcist

According to the New Testament, any baptized Christian can perform an exorcism. But no matter what his or her training or

This drawing depicts Jesus driving out a mute's demon. Many of Jesus' miracles in the New Testament were exorcisms.

background, an exorcist performs what some say is a very difficult, dangerous job. The danger is reflected in the *Rituale Romanum,* or *Roman Ritual,* commissioned in 1614 by Pope Paul V. This instruction book for exorcisms—still in use today—is extremely comprehensive, with some rituals filling nearly forty pages. The *Rituale Romanum* warns that the exorcist is dealing with "an ancient and astute adversary, strong, and exceedingly evil" and the exorcist must have "a lively faith, an absolute confidence in God and Jesus."[48]

In this one-on-one battle against evil, the exorcist must be totally committed. He or she cannot quit no matter how horrible the experience. In the end, the exorcist must be the

Requirements for an Exorcist

According to Roman Catholic priest Montague Summers in *The History of Witchcraft and Demonology,* those performing exorcisms should conform to rigorous standards:

1. The priest or exorcist should be of mature age, humble, of blameless life, courageous, of experience, and well-attested prudence. . . .

2. He must be a man of scholarship and learning, a systematic student and well versed in the latest trends and developments of psychological science.

3. Possession is not . . . to be taken for granted. Each case is to be carefully examined and great caution to be used in distinguishing genuine possession from certain forms of disease.

4. He should admonish the possessed in so far as the latter is capable, to dispose himself for the exorcism by prayer, fasting, by confession, and Holy Communion. . . .

5. The exorcism should take place in the Church, or some other sacred place. . . . [No]

crowd of gazers must be suffered to assemble out of mere curiosity. . . .

6. If the patient seems to fall asleep . . . such actions are probably a ruse to trick him.

7. The exorcist . . . is to speak with command and authority, and should the patient be convulsed or tremble, let him be more fervent and more insistent. . . .

8. Let the exorcist remember that he uses the words of Holy Scripture and Holy Church, not his own words and phrases.

9. All idle and impertinent questioning of the demon is to be avoided, nor should the evil spirit be allowed to speak at length unchecked and unrebuked.

10. The Blessed Sacrament is not to be brought near the body of the obsessed during exorcism for fear of possible irreverence. . . .

11. If expulsion of the evil spirit, who will often prove obstinate, is not secured at once, the rite should be repeated as often as need be.

winner, and Satan must be defeated. Even if the exorcist wins, however, it is said that he or she will forever bear the wounds of the diabolical confrontation, as Martin writes:

> [The exorcist] must consent to a dreadful and irreparable pillage of his deepest self. Something dies in him. Some part of his humanness will wither from such close contact with the opposite of all humanness—the essence of evil; and it is rarely if ever revitalized. No return will be made to him for his loss. . . . If he loses in the fight with Evil Spirit, he has an added penalty. He may or may not ever again perform the rite of Exorcism, but he must finally confront and vanquish the evil spirit that repulsed him. [49]

Those who take on such harrowing missions tend to be older priests, between the ages of fifty and sixty-five. These men need not be scholars but must possess strong moral authority and unwavering religious convictions. And as Oesterreich states: "Women and children should be excluded [from exorcisms], as well as the vulgar curious." [50]

No formal classes exist to train exorcists. Oftentimes the priest begins as an assistant and receives "on the job training" by someone who has previously performed exorcisms. As an assistant, the priest may help the exorcist by monitoring the proceedings. The assistant is also expected to take over if the lead priest tires, collapses, becomes hysterical, runs away, or even dies from the exertion. All such behavior has occurred during exorcisms.

Laypersons may also be present at exorcisms. These people might be professionals, such as medical doctors or psychiatrists. Close family members may also attend. Because victims may become violent and even allegedly possess superhuman strength, exorcists look for lay attendees who possess above-average physical strength. Like the exorcist himself, these witnesses must be of strong moral authority, because they

A Catholic archbishop performs an exorcism in 2002. Exorcists must adhere to rigorous standards of conduct.

too might be ostensibly attacked by the devil. Martin adds more details about attendees at an exorcism:

> The exorcist must be as certain as possible beforehand that his assistants will not be weakened or overcome by obscene behavior or by language foul beyond their imagining; they cannot blanch at blood, excrement, urine; they must be able to take awful personal insults and be prepared to have their darkest secrets screeched in public in front of their companions. These are routine happenings during exorcisms.
>
> Assistants . . . [must] obey the exorcist's commands immediately and without question, no matter how absurd

or unsympathetic those commands may appear to them to be . . . and they are never to speak to the possessed person, even by way of exclamation. [51]

Preparing for an Exorcism

Although every diabolical possession is said to be different, exorcists tend to follow specific routines when allegedly "casting out the devil" from a victim. First and foremost, the exorcist needs to be sure that the victim is in the throes of diabolical possession. Most of the time the person possessed is actually suffering from a mental or physical illness. This is most often the case according to French priest and exorcist Henri Gesland, who says "there have only been four cases of what I believe to be demonic possession"[52] out of three thousand recorded cases that he studied.

In past centuries, exorcisms were only conducted in churches or some other holy place. Today it is considered most favorable for the exorcism to take place out of the public eye, in the victim's home or that of a close relative or friend. Most often the room is one that may provide a special comfort to the possessed, such as his or her bedroom or living room. Since exorcisms are often violent, the room must be cleared of most furniture and objects that could be thrown, broken, or moved about by Satan. This involves removing couches, tables, chairs, and lamps and taking down curtains, pictures, and even chandeliers. In fact, only two pieces of furniture are recommended: a single bed or couch where the possessed can sit or lie down and a small table next to the bed to hold a crucifix, holy water, and anointing oils. Exorcist Ken Olson explains why these symbols are important:

> I often use a crucifix in [an] exorcism. . . . I've discovered that Satan absolutely hates it. Demons don't like to look at the crucifix, and it seems to agitate them so much that they want to leave. Holy water is another device that can be powerful in the battle. . . . I offer my

client a glass of this water blessed by the Spirit, and demons react quickly. Often they will leave when it is consumed. The more powerful the demons, the stronger their reactions will be to holy water, the crucifix, or anointing oil that has been blessed by the Holy Spirit. Demons sometimes recoil as if burned when touched by these holy objects.[53]

In addition to sacred objects, tape recorders and video cameras are sometimes present to record the exorcism. CD players can also be utilized to play religious music.

Because the victim might try to escape, doors must be locked and windows should be completely blocked with securely nailed plywood boards. This also provides protection for the exorcists and assistants who might be propelled through the window by the sheer spiritual force of the devil. Many times physical restraints such as straitjackets, ropes, or leather straps are kept close by to prevent escape or physical violence.

Attention is also given to the exorcists' wardrobe. For Catholic priests, each must wear the traditional long cassock that covers them from neck to foot. Over this a white surplice is worn with a narrow purple stole around the neck.

The exorcism begins when the person to be exorcized is brought into the room. It cannot end until the devil is vanquished. Sometimes this may be accomplished in only a few hours; other times the ritual can last up to a week. Most exorcisms take at least twelve hours. In rare cases, however, the exorcist cannot finish his or her work in one continuous session, as the exorcism can take months or even years.

Before any exorcism can begin, the possessed person must be prepared for the often disturbing events expected to follow. The victim must believe that he or she can be healed and understand that the exorcism can be successful only with an unquestioning faith. He or she must also be warned of the physical trauma that might ensue. As Olson writes: "There may sometimes be feelings of nausea and actual vomiting. Sometimes

The demon possessing this girl reacts strongly to a crucifix. Sacred objects often help to drive out demons.

the demons exit through a mass of phlegm or mucous expelled through the mouth. It helps to keep on hand some tissues . . . and a wastebasket, which we sometimes jokingly call a 'demon bucket.'"[54] Victims may also experience terrifying choking or horrifying pains in the chest, head, or other vital areas of the body.

The Ritual

Exorcisms begin with prayer, and the *Rituale Romanum* contains the oldest instructions for the process. Most handbooks

The *Rituale Romanum*

The *Rituale Romanum* is the only formal exorcism rite sanctioned by the Roman Catholic Church. It was written in 1614 under Pope Paul V. These words are to be chanted by the exorcist when casting out the devil:

> I exorcise you, most vile spirit, the very incarnation of our adversary, the specter, the enemy, in the name of Jesus Christ to get out and flee from this creature of God. He himself commands you who ordered you thrown from the heights of heaven to the depths of the earth. He commands you, who rules the sea, the winds and the tempests. Hear, therefore, and shudder, O Satan, you enemy of the Faith, enemy of the human race, cause of death, thief of life, destroyer of justice, source of evils, root of vice, seducer of men, betrayer of nations, source of jealousy, origin of avarice, cause of discord, procurer of sorrows—why do you remain and resist when you know that Jesus Christ blocks your plans? Fear him who in Isaac was immolated, who was sold in Joseph, who was killed in the lamb, who was crucified in man and then became the conqueror of hell. . . .

> Most vile dragon, in the name of the immaculate lamb, who trod upon the asp and the basilisk [legendary serpent], who conquered the lion and the dragon, I command you to get out of this man, to get out of the Church of God. Tremble and flee at that name which Hell fears; that name to which the virtues of heaven, the powers and the dominations are subject, which the cherubim and seraphim praise with untiring voices, chanting, Holy, Holy, Holy, Lord God of Sabaoth.

for exorcists in print today are based on this seventeenth-century text. The rite alternates prayers and words to be chanted during an exorcism. In five parts, the ritual proceeds as prayer, exorcism, prayer, exorcism, prayer. This sequence is often interrupted by readings from Scriptures, however. Oesterreich comments on the structure of the ritual:

> From the psychological point of view this construction is by no means inept. While the exorcism seeks to work upon the "demon" by threats and commands, the prayers are designed to help the possessed person, reinforcing his desire to be delivered by the demon, and increasing his confidence in the divine power which is invoked. [55]

During the reading of this or similar rites, the exorcist often makes the sign of the cross, sprinkles holy water, and wraps his stole around the exorcee.

Unlike a psychiatrist, who addresses a patient and offers suggestions for a cure, the exorcist never tells the victim that he or she should cast out the demon. Instead, the exorcist always speaks directly to the devil, commanding him to leave or offering to convert him to Christianity. When the devil is finally defeated, Justinus Kerner writes, the "cure is produced magically by prayer and conjurations, and chiefly by the name of Jesus pronounced with an assured faith."[56]

The Six Dramatic Stages

While the basics of an exorcism can sound deceptively simple, the experience is anything but mundane. The ritual takes

In this scene from The Exorcist, *the exorcist uses the* Rituale Romanum *to expel the demon.*

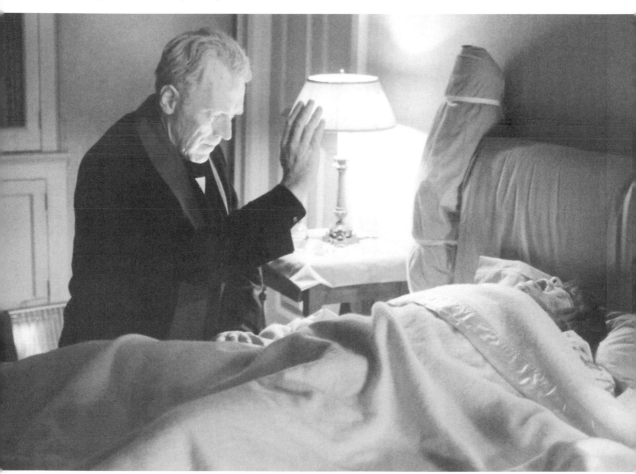

place in what some describe as a battle to the death with evil. According to Martin, the exorcist must be aware of six dramatic phases of exorcism that indicate progress. These are described as presence, pretense, breakpoint, voice, clash, and expulsion.

In the presence phase, all the attendees can feel the company of Satan from the moment they gather in the room for the exorcism. While the presence cannot be seen, photographed, or recorded with electronic instruments, the presence of evil is undeniable. Described as a hiss in the brain or a hateful vibration, this presence often causes immediate panic as the exorcism begins.

Pretense is the term that describes the efforts of the evil spirit to "hide" within the exorcee, as if the victim and victimizer were one in the same. During the pretense phase, the devil may speak through the victim or simply remain silent. If he does speak, according to Martin,

> [he] may speak with the voice of the possessed, and use past experiences and recollections of the possessed. This is often done skillfully, using details no one but the possessed could know. It can be very disarming, even pitiful. It can make everyone, including the priest, feel that it is the priest who is the villain, subjecting an innocent person to terrible rigors. Even the mannerisms and characteristics of the possessed are used by the spirit as its own camouflage. . . .
>
> Every exorcist learns during *Pretense* that he is dealing with some force or power that is at times intensely cunning, sometimes supremely intelligent, and at other times capable of crass stupidity . . . and it is both highly dangerous and terribly vulnerable.[57]

The main job of the exorcist at this point is to force the evil spirit to reveal itself, or to come out of hiding. This is often the most difficult and time-consuming phase of the exorcism, but until pretense occurs the ritual cannot proceed.

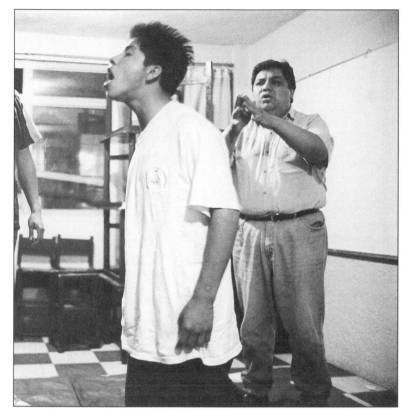

A possessed youth cries out during an exorcism. Such vocalizations indicate one of the six phases of an exorcism.

Breakpoint, Voicing, Clashing, and Expulsion

The attendees understand that the pretense phase is drawing to a close when the victim unleashes a stream of obscenities, abuse, violence, bodily fluids, and other physical horrors. This shows that the devil knows he is losing the fight. At this time the breakpoint begins, as the demon breaks or separates from its victim and becomes a terrifying physical being to be reckoned with on its own.

At this point weird supernatural experiences are said to scramble the senses of the attendees. They might be able to smell words, see sounds, or taste the guttural noises made by Satan. This jumbling of the senses can make the exorcist feel as if they are going insane.

The breakpoint is followed by the voice phase. During this period, the voice of the victim changes from his or her own to that of the demon. The voice of Satan can allegedly play many tricks on the attendees. It is said to be an alien noise that may sound like a tape recording alternating on slow and fast speeds. It can be painfully loud, or it can be whisper quiet. Words may have no meaning or may be used in poetic incantations that reveal intimate details from the lives of the attendees. Screaming, laughing, groaning, and other sounds may also accompany the words. The voice phase constitutes another battle of wits with Satan, who must be ordered to silence himself. Various methods may be employed to quiet the demon, including the playing of loud gospel music, prayers, and direct commands to shut up.

If the exorcist is successful, and the voice is silenced, the next phase of the exorcism begins. This is a war of wills between the exorcist and the evil spirit known as the clash. In this phase, the presence of the victim and other attendees becomes insignificant as the exorcist and the devil communicate without using words. As the exorcist attempts to harness the will of God to defeat the evil spirit, the devil tries to invade the body and soul of his enemy and take possession of the exorcist. Martin describes what the exorcist must accomplish during the clash phase:

> The issue between the two, the exorcist and the possessing spirit, is simple. Will the totally antihuman invade and take over? Will [the devil], noisome and merciless, seep over that narrow rim where the exorcist would hold his ground alone, and engulf him? Or will it, unwillingly, protestingly, under a duress greater than its single-track will, stop, identify itself, cede, retire, disappear, and [evaporate] back into an unknown pit of being where no man wants to go ever?
>
> Even with all the pressure on him, and in fullest human agony, if the exorcist has got this far, he must press home. He has gained an advantage. He has already forced the evil spirit to come out on its own. . . . And

then, some exorcists feel, the exorcist must pursue for as much information as he can. For in some peculiar way, as exorcists find, the more an evil spirit can be forced to reveal in the *Clash* and its aftermath, the surer and easier will be the *Expulsion* when that moment comes. To force as complete an identification as possible is perhaps a mark of domination of one will over another. [58]

The clash constitutes the most violent phase of the exorcism. Having identified himself and possibly losing a wordless battle against godly powers, the devil punishes the exorcee with unimaginable tortures. Violent expulsion of bodily fluids from the possessed, including vomit and phlegm, usually accompany this phase. The soul, too, is said to become polluted as the possessed person's mind fills with thoughts of despair, hatred, cruelty, contempt, and even madness. At this time, if the exorcist prevails, he will command the devil to cease and desist his possession of the victim, to depart, and go back to hell.

If this phase, known as expulsion, is successful, the atmosphere in the room will change instantly. The growls, shrieks, and cackling of the devil will fade away into silence. Those who have experienced an expulsion compare it to waking up and blinking away a long nightmare. Sometimes the victim will have memories of the possession; many times he or she will not. The exorcist will, however, remember every gruesome detail. In the weeks, months, and years that follow, he or she might face depression, insomnia, nightmares, flashbacks, and other symptoms as if he had been in combat. Most consider these conditions to be occupational hazards gleaned from having waged a triumphant battle of righteousness against the ultimate evil.

Are Exorcisms Real?

Even with all the negative consequences allegedly in store for an exorcist, an increasing number of exorcisms are performed every year. Even Pope John Paul revealed in 2002 that he himself had performed three exorcisms since 1982. Theologians have blamed the worldwide increase in exorcisms on widespread ignorance of the Bible and a growth in spiritual confusion among the young.

Even as the number of exorcisms grows, however, the Vatican has issued revised guidelines for expelling demons. In

Increasing numbers of exorcisms impelled the Catholic Church to issue a revised exorcism rite in 1999, shown here by a Vatican spokesman.

1999, for the first time since the *Rituale Romanum* was published, exorcists have been urged to avoid mistaking psychiatric illness for possession. The guidelines also warn against those who are faking possession, victims of their own imagination.

Modern historians who have studied exorcisms throughout the centuries have discovered that most alleged demonization can be blamed on other causes. For example, psychologists have said that people have historically feigned possession in order to act out sexual frustrations, escape unpleasant duties, attract attention, garner sympathy, or protest a disagreeable living situation. And mental illness is by far the most widespread catalyst for claims of demonic possession. Therefore, according to the New England Skeptical Society Web site:

> Exorcism is a very dangerous practice, not because of the involvement of [the devil], but because it feeds into the victim's delusions. There have been many documented cases where psychotic patients have declared themselves possessed, and act in accordance with the fables of being possessed (vile language, blasphemy and convulsive violence). When an exorcist declares them possessed, it feeds directly into their delusion, and drives the poor soul deeper into fantasy, and further from lucidity. All during this time, real psychological counseling is absent, and the victim is left to the whims of the exorcist. In all such cases, no genuine supernatural knowledge or abilities have been demonstrated by the alleged victim. Their behavior is consistent with someone who is merely psychotic.[59]

When Exorcisms Kill

Whether or not exorcisms are real, alleged victims of demonic possession have been killed by overzealous exorcists. Dozens of such incidents have been described in news accounts. In

A Skeptical Look at Exorcism

There are many who doubt the reality of diabolical possession and exorcism. Robert Todd Carroll, author of the following article "Exorcism" from the Skeptic's Dictionary Web site believes that both the exorcist and exorcized are simply engaged in self-deception:

> Reverend Brian Connor, of South Carolina. . . . was featured on NBC's "Dateline" program on exorcism (November 13, 2001). He and several friends spent an entire day trying to talk the demons out of the body of a 50-something man with a history of depression and aimlessness. The exorcists held Bibles, which they read from occasionally, and crosses. They huddled around their subject for hours, chanting prayers and ordering the demons to leave. The subject occasionally howled like an animal and grimaced at his benefactors. It was all great drama and eventually cathartic enough for the subject to vomit a little. Connor declared that he was spitting out Satan and that all the demons had left. . . .
>
> I found the behavior of the exorcists at least as interesting as that of the subject. Believing in demons is one thing; believing you have the ability to call up a supernatural being with infinite power and perfection who will cause demons to move on at your behest, seems [crazy]. The whole coven of exorcists and exorcized are deluded. The [exorcists] clearly felt great pride at their achievement and shared in a glorious victory over Satan. The [exorcized] was coddled and cuddled, hugged and loved, and eventually praised and rewarded with the good feelings of caring people when he released Satan and said "Jesus is Lord." There doesn't seem to be anything deeply complicated about what happened. The group convinced the subject he was possessed. They cued him as to how to behave and they rewarded him and themselves when he let the demon go.

1997, for example, a Christian woman was stomped to death in Glendale, California, as exorcists attempted to drive the devil from her body. In another case that same year, a five-year-old New York City girl was force-fed a poisonous mixture of ammonia and vinegar by deluded exorcists trying to expel Satan.

In an August 2003 case more reminiscent of the Middle Ages than the twenty-first century, an eight-year-old Milwaukee boy suffocated to death after his chest was tightly wrapped in sheets during an exorcism. The exorcism was held because the child had severe autism. This meant he could barely speak and had difficulties relating to people around him. His condition, however, was diagnosed by members of the Temple Church of the Apostolic Faith to be diabolical possession.

Such exorcisms have harmed countless people throughout the ages. But with few records, there is no way of knowing how many were helped by exorcists. Like all issues of possession, belief in exorcism is a matter of faith. While the reality of curing demonization remains a mystery, it is likely that exorcisms will continue to be performed well into the foreseeable future.

Notes

Introduction: What Is Possession?

1. Malachi Martin, *Hostage to the Devil.* San Francisco: HarperCollins, 1992, pp. 10–11.

Chapter 1: Spirit Possession Throughout History

2. Quoted in Justine Glass, *They Foresaw the Future.* New York: G.P. Putnam's Sons, 1969, p. 42.
3. Glass, *They Foresaw the Future*, p. 39.
4. Quoted in Glass, *They Foresaw the Future*, p. 40.
5. William Sargant, *The Mind Possessed.* Philadelphia: J.B. Lippincott, 1974, p. 62.
6. Quoted in Roger Baker, *Binding the Devil.* New York: Hawthorn Books, 1974, p. 13.
7. Baker, *Binding the Devil*, p. 56.
8. Gary K. Waite, *Heresy, Magic, and Witchcraft in Early Modern Europe.* New York: Palgrave Macmillan, 2003, p. 165.
9. D.P. Walker, *Unclean Spirits.* Philadelphia: University of Pennsylvania Press, 1981, p. 10.
10. Théodore Flournoy, *From India to the Planet Mars: A Study of a Case of Somnambulism with Glossolalia.* New York: Harper & Brothers, 1900, p. 117.
11. Quoted in James Houran and Rense Lange, eds., *Hauntings and Poltergeists.* Jefferson, NC: McFarland, 2001, p. 248.

Chapter 2: Worldwide Possession

12. Erika Bourguignon, *Possession.* San Francisco: Chandler & Sharp, 1976, p. 17.
13. Bourguignon, *Possession*, pp. 20–21.
14. Sargant, *The Mind Possessed*, p. 181.
15. Barbara Placido, "It's All To Do with Words: An Analysis of Spirit Possession in the Venezuelan Cult of Maria Lionza," *Journal of the Royal Anthropological Institute*, June 2001, p. 213.
16. Placido, "It's All to Do with Words," p. 218.
17. Didier Bertrand, "The Names and Identities of the Boramey Spirits Possessing Cambodian Mediums," *Asian Folklore Studies*, April 2001, p. 36.
18. Bertrand, "The Names and Identities of the Boramey Spirits Possessing Cambodian Mediums," p. 37.
19. Bertrand, "The Names and Identities of the Boramey Spirits Possessing Cambodian Mediums," pp. 33–34.
20. Bertrand, "The Names and Identities of the Boramey Spirits Possessing Cambodian Mediums," p. 44.

Chapter 3: Possessed by Poltergeists

21. Quoted in Allan Kardec, *The Spirits' Book.* São Paulo, Brazil: Lake, 1989, p. 229.

22. Quoted in Kardec, *The Spirits' Book*, p. 230.

23. Colin Wilson, *Poltergeist: A Study in Destructive Haunting*. St. Paul, MN: Llewellyn, 1993, pp. 256–57.

24. Quoted in Colin Wilson, *Poltergeist*, p. 259.

25. Quoted in Wilson, *Poltergeist*, p. 264.

26. Quoted in Wilson, *Poltergeist*, p. 264.

27. Wilson, *Poltergeist*, p. 44.

28. Wilson, *Poltergeist*, p. 394.

Chapter Four: Diabolical Possession

29. T.K. Oesterreich, *Possession Demoniacal & Other*, Seacaucus, NJ: University Books, 1966, p. 199.

30. Quoted in Oesterreich, *Possession Demoniacal & Other*, p. 22.

31. Quoted in Adolf Rodewyk, *Possessed by Satan*. Garden City, NY: Doubleday, 1975, p. 139.

32. Rodewyk, *Possessed by Satan*, p. 140.

33. Rodewyk, *Possessed by Satan*, p. 143.

34. Ken Olson, *Exorcism: Fact or Fiction?* Nashville, TN: Thomas Nelson, 1992, p. 125.

35. Olson, *Exorcism*, p. 123.

36. Martin, *Hostage to the Devil*, p. 437.

37. Olson, *Exorcism*, p. 123.

38. Martin, *Hostage to the Devil*, p. 436.

39. Martin, *Hostage to the Devil*, p. 439.

40. Quoted in Martin, *Hostage to the Devil*, p. 441.

41. Quoted in Mark Chorvinsky, "The Haunted Boy of Cottage City," 1999. *Strange Magazine*, www.strangemag.com/exorcistpage1.html.

42. Chorvinsky, "The Haunted Boy of Cottage City."

43. Quoted in Chorvinsky, "The Haunted Boy of Cottage City."

44. Chorvinsky, "The Haunted Boy of Cottage City."

Chapter Five: Exorcising the Devil

45. Baker, *Binding the Devil*, p. 37.

46. Walker, *Unclean Spirits*, p. 4.

47. Baker, *Binding the Devil*, p. 102.

48. Quoted in Oesterreich, *Possession Demoniacal & Other*, p. 102.

49. Martin, *Hostage to the Devil*, p. 10.

50. Quoted in Oesterreich, *Possession Demoniacal & Other*, p. 102.

51. Martin, *Hostage to the Devil*, p. 16.

52. Quoted in Martin, *Hostage to the Devil*, p. 11.

53. Olson, *Exorcism*, p. 146.

54. Olson, *Exorcism*, p. 148.

55. Oesterreich, *Possession Demoniacal & Other*, p. 103.

56. Quoted in Oesterreich, *Possession Demoniacal & Other*, p. 105.

57. Martin, *Hostage to the Devil*, p. 18–19.

58. Martin, *Hostage to the Devil*, p. 21.

59. The New England Skeptical Society, "Exorcism," www.theness.com/encyc/exorcism-encyc.htm.

For Further Reading

Books

Gary L. Blackwood, *Paranormal Powers*. New York: Benchmark Books, 1999. Discusses ESP, enhanced perception, PK energy, and other paranormal phenomena that have been traced to spirit possession.

Felicitas D. Goodman, *How About Demons?* Bloomington: Indiana University Press, 1988. A study of possessions and exorcism in modern times with an exploration of the phenomena in various religions and cultures throughout the world.

Peter Hepplewhite and Neil Tonge. *Hauntings*. London: Egmont Childrens Books, 1997. Discusses ghostly phenomena, poltergeist activity, and other unexplained mysteries.

Patricia D. Netzley, *Haunted Houses*. San Diego: Lucent Books, 2000. An exploration of the tricks, mischief, and scary phenomena attributed to ghosts and poltergeists in haunted houses.

Terry O'Neill, ed., *Ghosts and Poltergeists*. San Diego: Greenhaven Press, 2002. A compilation of articles by experts in paranormal phenomena that explore the myths and realities of undead spirits.

Internet Sources

Trent Brandon, "Ghosts, Hauntings, & Poltergeists," Zerotime, 2004. www.zerotime.com/ghosts/.

Robert Todd Carroll, "Exorcism," The Skeptic's Dictionary, 2002. http://skepdic.com/exorcism.html.

Works Consulted

Books

Roger Baker, *Binding the Devil.* New York: Hawthorn Books, 1974. A history of the devil, possession, and exorcism with an analysis of the rise in such beliefs following the release of the film *The Exorcist.*

Erika Bourguignon, *Possession.* San Francisco: Chandler & Sharp, 1976. A study of voluntary spirit possession in cultures throughout the world.

Richard Cavendish, *The World of Ghosts and the Supernatural.* New York: Facts On File, 1994. A study of the occult and unexplained phenomenon, including ghosts and hauntings, from various cultures around the world.

Martin Ebon, *The Devil's Bride: Exorcism: Past and Present.* New York: Harper & Row, 1974. Case histories of possessions and exorcisms in cultures throughout the world, with explanations that deal in psychology, religious belief, and other causes.

Théodore Flournoy, *From India to the Planet Mars: A Study of a Case of Somnambulism with Glossolalia.* New York: Harper & Brothers, 1900. A five-year psychological study of medium Hélène Smith, who claimed to channel the spirit of magician Leopold Cagliostro and others.

Justine Glass, *They Foresaw the Future.* New York: G.P. Putnam's Sons, 1969. A historic account of six thousand years of prophecy from ancient Egypt to well-known twentieth-century predictors such as Edgar Cayce and Jeanne Dixon.

Rosemary Ellen Guiley, *Harper's Encyclopedia of Mystical & Paranormal Experience.* Edison, NJ: Castle Books, 1991. A comprehensive compilation of more than five hundred supernatural experiences and people involved in psychic phenomena, with history, explanations, and techniques explained.

James Houran and Rense Lange eds., *Hauntings and Poltergeists.* Jefferson, NC: McFarland, 2001. A study of the cultural, physical, and psychological aspects of ghosts written by the world's leading authorities.

Allan Kardec, *The Spirits' Book.* São Paulo, Brazil: Lake, 1989. An 1857 book compiled from fifty notebooks containing transcripts and journals of numerous spirit communications, supplemented with answers to philosophical and scientific questions the author posed to different mediums in different countries. Written under the pen name Allan Kardec by French spiritualist H. Leon Denizard Rivail.

Heinrich Krämer and Jakob Sprenger, *Malleus Maleficarum.* New York: B. Blom, 1970. A manual written by two German Dominican friars in 1486 that was used to identify, persecute, and execute witches and was blamed for setting off a wave of witch hysteria that resulted in the deaths of more than one hundred thousand people falsely accused of witchcraft.

Malachi Martin, *Hostage to the Devil.* San Francisco: HarperCollins, 1992. A study of the alleged possession and exorcism of five Americans written by an eminent theologian and authority on the Roman Catholic Church.

T.K. Oesterreich, *Possession Demoniacal & Other.* Seacaucus, NJ: University Books, 1966. First published in Germany in 1921, this book explores demonic and spirit possession in antiquity, the Middle Ages, and modern times.

Ken Olson, *Exorcism: Fact or Fiction?* Nashville, TN: Thomas Nelson, 1992. The author, a Lutheran minister, psychologist, and practicing exorcist, leaves little doubt that he believes diabolical possession is very real—and often the result of people toying with New Age spiritualism, games such as Dungeons and Dragons, and even Tarot cards.

A.R.G. Owen, *Can We Explain the Poltergeist?* New York: Helix Press, 1964. A scientific explanation of poltergeists, with chapters about real, fake, and unexplainable manifestations.

Pope Paul V, *Rituale Romanum.* Regensburg, Germany: Fredrick Pustet, 1925. Written in 1614, this book remains today the only guidebook for procedures to be followed by exorcists that is officially sanctioned by the Roman Catholic Church.

Adolf Rodewyk, *Possessed by Satan.* Garden City, NY: Doubleday, 1975. Originally published in Germany in 1963, this book covers the church's teaching on the devil, possession, and exorcism.

William Sargant, *The Mind Possessed.* Philadelphia: J.B. Lippincott, 1974. A scientific, cultural, and historical examination of spirit possession, mysticism, and faith healing.

Montague Summers, *The History of Witchcraft and Demonology.* New York: Alfred A. Knopf, 1926. A book by a Roman Catholic priest concerning religion, witches, devils, and possession from ancient times to the modern era.

Gary K. Waite, *Heresy, Magic, and Witchcraft in Early Modern Europe.* New York: Palgrave Macmillan, 2003. A study of the fifteenth-century connection among heresy, witchcraft, and demonic possession and exorcism.

D.P. Walker, *Unclean Spirits.* Philadelphia: University of Pennsylvania Press, 1981. A history of possession and exorcism in France and England in the sixteenth and seventeenth centuries.

Colin Wilson, *Poltergeist: A Study in Destructive Haunting.* St. Paul, MN: Llewellyn, 1993. Examples of hostile ghosts and negative psychic phenomena as a result of black magic, psychokinesis, fairies, and other causes.

Periodicals

Didier Bertrand, "The Names and Identities of the Boramey Spirits Possessing Cambodian Mediums," *Asian Folklore Studies,* April 2001.

Barbara Placido, "It's All to Do with Words: An Analysis of Spirit Possession in the Venezuelan Cult of Maria Lionza," *Journal of the Royal Anthropological Institute,* June 2001.

Piers Vitebsky, "Dialogues with the Dead." *Natural History,* March 1997.

Internet Sources

Bible.com, "Acts 10," http://bibleontheweb.com/Bible.asp, (no date). The Bible on the Web, including the full Old and New Testaments.

Mark Chorvinsky, "The Haunted Boy of Cottage City," *Strange Magazine,* 1999.

www.strangemag.com/exorcistpage1.html.

The New England Skeptical Society, "Exorcism," www.theness.com/encyc/exorcism-encyc.html.

Joe Nickell, "Exorcism! Driving Out the Nonsense," Committee for the Scientific Investigation of Claims of the Paranormal (CSICOP), January/February, 2001. www.csicop.org/si/2001-01/i-files.html.

WholeHealthMD.com, "Native American Medicine," 2004. www.wholehealthmd.com/refshelf/substances_view/1,1525,721,00.html.

Index

Picture Credits

Cover Image: AP/Wide World Photos
AP/Wide World Photos, 39, 40, 66, 92
© Archivo Iconografico, S.A./CORBIS, 11, 18
© Thony Belizaire/AFP/Getty Images, 31, 34
© Laurie Berger/Mary Evans Picture Library, 49
© Bettmann/CORBIS, 23, 46, 61, 73, 76, 87
© Keith Dannemiller/CORBIS, 9, 89
© Joseph Fabry/Time Life Pictures/Getty Images, 36
© Fortean Picture Library, 14, 24, 54, 68, 85
© Historical Picture Archive/CORBIS, 79
© Mary Evans Picture Library, 57
© Franco Origlia/Getty Images, 82
© Guy Lyon Playfair/Fortean Picture Library, 52

About the Author

Stuart A. Kallen is the author of more than 170 nonfiction books for children and young adults. He has written on topics ranging from the theory of relativity to the history of rock and roll. In addition, Kallen has written award-winning children's videos and television scripts. In his spare time, Kallen is a singer/songwriter/guitarist in San Diego, California.